The Jewish Singularity

The Jewish Singularity

✦

Genes, Memes, and Mystery

Avri Barr

iUniverse, Inc.
New York Lincoln Shanghai

The Jewish Singularity
Genes, Memes, and Mystery

iUniverse books may be ordered through booksellers or by contacting:

iUniverse
2021 Pine Lake Road, Suite 100
Lincoln, NE 68512
www.iuniverse.com
1-800-Authors (1-800-288-4677)

ISBN-13: 978-0-595-40625-8 (pbk)
ISBN-13: 978-0-595-84992-5 (ebk)
ISBN-10: 0-595-40625-4 (pbk)
ISBN-10: 0-595-84992-X (ebk)

Printed in the United States of America

Contents

Acknowledgements

Faith, history, and genetics are such fascinating and interwoven subjects that they should be dealt with as a hobby, not an occupation. This was what I did, attempting to complement my expertise in exact science and engineering. In this regard, the amazing books by Paul Johnson about Jewish history, Ricky Lewis about human genetics, and Karen Armstrong about three monotheistic faiths provided both inspiration and knowledge.

My long-time friend Charles Bert, professor of the University of Oklahoma in Norman, sparked my interest in systematic studies of Jewish history. The invitation to spend my sabbatical with the Department of Physics, School of Electrical and Communication Engineering, Brno University of Technology, extended by professors Lubomir Grmela and Karel Liedermann, enabled me to enjoy Czech hospitality and to literally follow in the footsteps of the father of genetics, Gregor Mendel, at the Augustinian Abbey of St. Thomas in Brno. Assa Lifshitz, professor of the Hebrew University of Jerusalem, has let me benefit from his outstanding appreciation of human nature.

Finally, I owe thanks to Diana, Ruth, Lior, Ronni, and Gil for bringing so much joy into my life.

Preface

Winter nights in Kiev, the Ukrainian capital, are cold and windy, but tired of traveling in a smelly coach, I decided to get out of the station building and catch a spurt of fresh air before going on to my next destination. It was around 3 AM, and the large front square was empty; sparsely placed lights failed to provide minimal illumination. I noticed the fuzzy figures of two men passing by about thirty meters from me, and overheard one of them saying "Do you see that Jew over there?". Back on my seat in the coach, I tried to analyze the incident. Let us assume for a moment that my facial features or posture give away my Jewish origins; still, because of the darkness, the distance, and the bulky winter dress I was wearing, it would be absolutely impossible to notice those. So, how exactly is it that that man has "calculated" me as a Jew? It was clearly a puzzle. Presumably, the man had caught my "otherness" by his senses; in the Soviet Union there was only one "other" world, it was the Jewish world. I had heard similar stories from my Jewish acquaintances of those times; one of whom was an athletically built young man with blue eyes and red hair, far removed from a familiar Jewish stereotype.

Each nation is unique in its own way. What is it that makes Jewish people unique? Virtually everything concerning the Jews is complicated and controversial. They are both a nation and a religion, at the same time. Like chameleons, they may take on any identity, be it Russian, American, German, Egyptian, or even Chinese, but they are almost always Jewish. They are spread over the world but worship a specific corner of Asia, which is also the meeting-point of Asia, Europe and Africa, called Canaan, Palestine or Israel, depending on the viewpoint. They excel as capitalists, communists, scientists, artists, terrorists, lawyers, revolutionaries, common criminals, musicians, spies, and physicians. They are a permanent focus of jokes and rumors. On top of that, they appear to have no challengers in longevity in that their origins can be traced as far back as three or perhaps four millennia.

The factors affecting the Jewish people throughout their long and mysterious history include the social *environment* they live in, *genes*, the biological units they inherit from their parents, and *memes*, the cultural and scientific units they pass on from generation to generation. Each of these will be presented in this book in an attempt to understand the Jewish phenomenon.

During the period of four millennia, from ancient to modern times, the Jews have been tested by a truly unique variety of social and geo-political surroundings, which have influenced their history but have left their spirituality and even language essentially untouched. Has their unequaled enduring capability and boldness followed from special Jewish genes or Jewish ideas, the memes?

Genetics, as a science, was pioneered by Gregor Mendel, who studied the hereditary traits of pea plants, such as the seed color. He explained his experimental results as the existence of special discrete factors, later to be called genes, which appear in pairs and are passed down from one generation to the next, thus replicating themselves. Genes, therefore, can be used as historic records.

A cultural analogy of the gene is the meme. The term was coined by Richard Dawkins in order to stress the replication phenomenon in culture and science, including traditions, habits and so forth, which may pass from person to person or from generation to generation. A good illustration is a stylish hair cut. The behavior is copied by one individual from another without the involvement of any genetic mechanism. In a broader sense, a meme is a piece of cultural or scientific information passing from one mind to another. Unlike genetics, which deals with specific biological mechanisms of heredity, memetics deals with a way of thinking over cultural and social issues, and is still a controversial subject; I will use the term mainly as a convenient means of discussing a variety of subjects in a single framework.

The main difference between genes and memes lies in the method of propagation: genes normally propagate by sexual intercourse, memes through signals, imitation, language, and media. Like genes, memes replicate, evolve, and mutate. Both may be lethal: genes can cause deadly diseases; memes can stimulate wars and revolutions. In a sense, humans are both gene and meme machines. Though not directly involved in the multiplication of our memes, our genes may influence their content; the meme of celibacy practiced by Catholic clergy, shows that our memes may affect our genes.

The Jewish tradition from ancient times up to the present was that there has been nothing genetic in the Jewish "otherness"; *it is not a genetic trait, like hair color.* The maximum that can be said is that recent studies have supplied evidence for common genetic characteristics of the Jewish people, preserved despite their dispersion among host nations over a period of two millennia; there are also theories trying to explain the fact of the enhanced intelligence of Jews as well as their hereditary disorders by a rare combination of social and genetic factors. However, no manifestations of a genetic gap between gentiles and Jews have been found. As to the memes, Jews, with their extraordinary spiritual, cultural, and scientific heritage, are perhaps the greatest meme machine.

There is no shortage of texts dealing with a systematic presentation of the Jewish history. One of them is a truly remarkable and fundamental study by Christian historian Paul Johnson. A recent book by Dean Hamer, which deals with an overlap of spirituality and genetics, was also an inspiration for me. This book is a multifaceted account of the Jewish experience, including its genetic, religious and cultural aspects, and the Jewish involvement in crucial historic events, which may help its readers to appreciate the nature of Jewish uniqueness.

1

History

The Jews…stand right at the centre of the perennial attempt to give human life the dignity of a purpose.

—Paul Johnson

Jews are here, Jews are there, Jews are almost everywhere, filling up the darkest places, evil looks upon their faces.

—Gideon Taylor, a boy of fourteen.

Is the Axis Jewish?

Does the world rotate around the Jewish axis? Vladimir Solovyev, a religious philosopher of the late nineteenth century, answered this question with an absolute "yes". I am far from being so definitive and would only claim that it deserves some discussion.

As a Russian story has it, there was a businessman who would not hire Jews to work at his company. When a guy named Abramowitz applied for a job, he was naturally turned down. Being a pure Russian, he approached the businessman, saying: "Believe me, I am not Jewish, even though my surname is Abramowitz", and got a reply: "Sorry, I still cannot hire you; if I hire Abramowitz, I would better hire a Jew". This gag clearly illustrates the duality and contradiction typical of the perception of the Jews; the same can be seen from the above epigraphs. It took the Jews at least three thousand years to earn their reputation.

Indeed, the Jewish people, champions of tenacity, began their recorded history that far back. Assuming a life expectancy of forty years, which was common for most of the period, this would amount to seventy five genera-

1

tions, but the world today still lives to a significant degree by Jewish traditions and laws. Common Christians and Muslims rarely realize the extent to which Jewish traditions influence their daily routine. If you took a look at a dollar bill, you could read "in God we trust"; this is the Jewish God in whom you trust. Jews standardized the now common pattern of seven days week including a compulsory resting day, which was a revolutionary idea for those times.

Most of the Christian or Muslim festivities cluster around the Jewish ones. Israelites were not the only ancient people who enforced dietary rules, but only they survived and preserved their language and traditions. Sometimes, memes perceived as explicitly gentile have Jewish origins: a typically American myth of Superman, indispensable to the American culture, was a creation of Joe Shuster and Jerry Siegel. The super-spy James Bond, a symbol of Anglo-Saxon perfection and vitality, was modeled by his author, Ian Fleming, after Sidney Reilly, born in Odessa, Russia, as Sigmund Rosenblum. He became an international adventurer and a prominent figure in the British Intelligence Service in the early twentieth century.

Jews discovered (some would say invented) the single all-mighty God, who was to become the common God of approximately thirteen million Jews, two billion Christians, and two billion Muslims presently leaving on planet Earth. The same Jews authored the Bible written with incomparable imagination, passion, and eloquent wording, full of hidden meanings and masterfully mixing realistic details and miracles. When the New Testament was added, it became probably the most published and influential book in the world. (In a peculiar way, the recently published list of books most frequently stolen from public libraries also displays the Bible as the first item.) Jews postulated the supremacy of the humans over all other living species, prohibited paganism and incest, and established the legal basis of civilized society in the form of the Ten Commandments.

The focus of the Old Testament was the Covenant between God and *His* (the Jewish) people. By this agreement from that time on nothing was to be taken for granted by the *chosen* people, especially the possession of land of their own, the land of Israel. This land would symbolize their ultimate possession; it would be the *Promised* Land, granted to the Jews with conditions attached. Materialization of this promise as well as the mere well-being of Jews would depend on a string of criteria to be fulfilled by them in a precise manner. In return, God would take special care of His people among all the other nations of the world. Obviously, the two parties involved were not equal: though God was all-mighty and absolutely perfect, the Jews were far from that. To make the Covenant even more peculiar, the Bible rarely applied rosy colors to the ancient Israelites; they were easily submitting to numerous human weaknesses and sins. From the very beginning, Israelites had difficulties sticking to the clauses of the Covenant and were therefore punished by God time and again.

As to the land of Israel (originally Canaan), in sharp contrast to surrounding countries, it lacks any significant natural resources; still, it is strategically located at the intersection of three continents, and, though small, has a variety of terrain, climate, and ecology. Was this land worthy of such fuss over so long a period of time? The peculiar and highly emotional attachment to a piece of land was a key element in preserving the Jewish identity. It is unique to Judaism, which is not racist in the genetic sense, but is, figuratively speaking, territorially "racist". Modern Israel has been at war with its neighbors for around sixty years. Yet, by a recent poll, over ninety percent of all Israelis would not buy peace, if they would have to give up their rights to the Western Wall, the surviving remnant of the Temple.

The story of Exodus from Egyptian slavery and the conquest of Canaan is another pillar of the Old Testament. Though historians still argue over the validity of the fact itself, a powerful description of the rebellion against the mighty master, the Pharaoh, and quest for freedom deeply affected the Jewish national character and, later on, Christianity and subsequent social movements.

Isaac Newton commented that "…if I have seen further it is by standing on the shoulders of Giants"; this is typical of the exact sciences to gratefully acknowledge contributions of the previous researchers. Christianity, though being the direct outgrowth of Judaism and owing a deep debt to the latter, rarely bothers to acknowledge it. Muslim clerics also try to blur the obvious Jewish foundations of Islam. That is why it is difficult to understand anti-Jewish feelings spread among Christian and Muslim communities. I could more easily interpret anti-Semitism originating out of atheism or paganism, both of which plainly reject God as a Jewish chimera. However, as critics of Christianity and Islam note, this is only human: first, one adopts what somebody else has created; second, he makes changes here and there, and then blackens the original to further amplify his own contribution and keep the glory solely for himself.

There is no rule without exceptions. One of the most influential personalities of the twentieth century, the late Pope John Paul II, born as Karol Jozef Wojtyla in a small Polish town, was an exception. Having the solid knowledge of the Soviet Empire from his own experience, he skillfully intrigued its dismantling behind the scenes. The assassination attempt on his life was apparently caused by this activity. The Pope, who, as a youth, had witnessed Nazi atrocities in his native Poland, tried to focus the relations between Christians and Jews on the Jewish uniqueness. He was the first Pope to visit both the Auschwitz death camp and a synagogue and declared the Jews to be "elder brothers". In 1993, the Vatican recognized Israel, sending a bold message to the world on the theological legitimacy of this state and even a hint of a possible realization of the Biblical prophecy. During his visit to Israel in 2000, the Pope, following a Jewish custom, placed a note in cracks of the Western Wall, calling for "genuine brotherhood with people of the Covenant". The same feelings were expressed much earlier, in 1816, by Napoleon: "It is my wish that the Jews be treated like brothers as if we were all part of Judaism". It is remarkable that this "Jews' Pope", as he was referred to, had grown up and lived for many years in an anti-Semitic environment typical of Eastern Europe.

The sheer magnitude of the time- and space-span of Jewish history appears to have no parallel. Having started three millennia ago at least, the Jewish people survived the destruction of their statehood and the Temple in the land of Israel (Canaan), exile, slavery, onslaught, pogroms, ghettos and Holocaust, managing to preserve their spiritual beliefs and language. Eventually the Jews, who just narrowly escaped extermination by the Nazis, in a surge of vitality, turned the tables and recovered their own statehood in the same very corner of the Earth from which they had been expelled two thousand years before; the ancient tribe sharpened its identity after two millennia of vagueness.

A few years ago, Charles Krauthammer, a media seer, commented in his typical silver-tongued manner that "Israel is the very embodiment of Jewish continuity: it is the only nation on earth that inhabits the same land, bears the same name, speaks the same language, and worships the same God that it did three thousand years ago. You dig the soil and you find pottery from Davidic times, coins from Bar Kochba, and two thousand year-old scrolls written in a script remarkably like the one that today advertises ice cream at the corner candy store." The same idea of the astonishing Jewish persistence was expressed by the historian, Paul Johnson: "If the earliest Jews were able to survey with us the history of their progeny, they would find nothing surprising in it."

Israel is still in the process of consolidation, going through the chain of wars with Arabs and is the focal point of widespread controversy. To a certain degree, anti-Zionists had set aside old-fashioned anti-Jewish feelings, especially in leftist circles, which claim that they have nothing against Jews but feel quite the opposite about the State of Israel. However, much of the pro-Palestinian movement sprang out of plain anti-Semitism: a problematic ethnic minority, defenseless for many centuries, made a turnabout, acquired independence and dared to resort to its own "iron fist" from time to time.

On the other hand, traditional white supremacists think of Israel as a handy opportunity for getting rid of the Jews by sending them off to the Promised Land. Hitler, they say, would also have preferred such a solution, if it had been available at the time. Israel's very existence is intolerable to Muslim extremists: Mohammed is the *last* prophet and therefore a Jewish state on the Muslim land is incompatible with the Holy Koran. Amazingly, they find understanding within Jewish ultra-Orthodox circles, which keep claiming that only God could recreate Israel, not mortal humans, and that Zionists committed a terrible sin by intervening in the divine plan. Around the Israeli issue you find a bizarre conglomerate in opposition: Islamic fundamentalists, Christian racists, Jewish ultra-Orthodox and leftist anarchists; these include various nationals, from a Malaysian cleric, to a Polish peasant, to a Californian student. By way of contrast, for conservative Christian movements it is as a fulfillment of the prophecy, a sign of the Second Coming of Christ.

Putting aside the Jewish collective heritage, it would be difficult to find fields of human activity without a significant influence of Jews as specific personalities. There is no need to detail the numerous names of outstanding Jewish figures that made major contributions to such divertive fields as art, science, media, technology, economy, politics, and social movements. A few years ago, the Israeli city of Rishon-Le-Zion began construction of a new neighborhood, intending to name each street after a Jewish Nobel Prize winner. Soon the municipality realized that this was not going to be easy: there was a severe shortage of streets. The Jewish Nobel Prize winners comprise around thirty percent of the whole.

One of the little known but spectacular flashes of Jewish creativeness took place in Hungary in the first half of the twentieth century. This country was a part of the Austro-Hungarian Empire which, being a loosely tailored conglomerate of nations provided a fruitful ground for inter-ethnic interaction and competition. Dennis Garbor, Edward Teller, Leo Szilard, John von Neumann, George de Hevesy and Paul Wigner were all born in Hungary more or less at the same time. Three of them received the Nobel Prize: Garbor for invention of the holography, Wigner for contributions to nuclear physics, and de Hevesy for his method of radioactive tracers. De Hevesy is also known for his use of chemistry in another remarkable way: he was in Denmark when it was invaded by the Nazis, he dissolved his Nobel gold medal in a solution and put the latter on a shelf; after the war, he precipitated gold out of the acid and later the medal was recovered by the Nobel Society. Szilard was probably the first to understand how the atomic bomb might work; together with Enrico Fermi he built the first atomic reactor. He wrote the text of the historic letter by Albert Einstein to President Franklin Roosevelt concerned with the possibility of building the atomic bomb and the danger that would arise as a result from Nazi Germany. This letter, whose effect was amplified later by the Japanese attack on Pearl Harbor, led to a head start of American research in atomic technology. Teller was especially instrumental in building up the American nuclear deterrence potential during the Cold War. Eventually, modern computer science would be impossible without the pioneering research of von Neumann. The astonishing success of the Jewish-Hungarian symbiosis seems to suggest that a multi-ethnic competitive environment contributed much to Jewish creativity.

Another unusual surge of Jewish excellence had its roots in the Russian Empire and Poland, this time in visual arts and music. Mark Chagall and Chaim Soutine were born into impoverished families struggling to survive under humiliating conditions of Jewish ghettos. Both of them became pillars of the modern visual arts, showing explicit Jewish motives in their paintings, in particular, the Hasidic culture that they were exposed to in their youth. Leon Bakst, born as Lev Rosenberg, debuted as a stage designer of the Hermitage, one of the greatest museums of the World, and the Aleksandrinskii Theatre in St. Petersburg in 1902, which brought him international fame. Later he was appointed artistic director of the *Ballets Russes,* and thereby, together with Serge Diaghilev, set the foundations for the unique Russian ballet. Jascha Heifetz, born in 1901 in Vilna, Lithuania, made his first public performance as a violinist at seven years of age and then became one of the greatest of all-time. Remarkably, he also wrote the popular hit "*When you make love to me, don't make believe*", hiding his song writing under the alias Jim Hoyl. Arthur Rubinstein debuted as a pianist in Berlin in 1900 when he was thirteen, and went on to become one of the best soloists of the twentieth century.

The vibrant spirit of poverty-stricken Jewish ghettos also produced a series of strange, if not bizarre, personalities of a special kind: the psychics. Wolf Messing, probably the most extraordinary, was born in Poland in 1899 and already, at the age of six, memorized the Talmud. As a penniless runaway of eleven, he arrived in Berlin where his unique talent, fraudulent or real, of "mind reading" came into play. He earned his living as a hypnotist and a fakir, his body being pierced with needles. He would also trace valuables purposely hidden by spectators. Messing performed all over the world, including Europe, Australia, Brazil, Japan, and India. He predicted in 1937 that "Hitler will die if he turns toward the East" and got a Nazi price of 200,000 marks put on his head; he also foresaw the date of his own death. In 1939, Germany started the Second World War by attacking Poland and, at the last moment, Messing fled from occupied Poland to Russia, where he died in 1974. There were rumours that Sigmund Freud, Albert Einstein, Mahatma Gandhi, and even Josef Stalin personally tested his psychic abilities. In one of those, Stalin requested that Messing show up in his office without the proper permits, which he did by convincing guards he was Lavrentii Beria, the feared security chief of Stalin.

It would be tedious at best, if at all possible, to go on and count the Jews who left their mark in the human history, for better or worse. Jews certainly have had a talent of being in the eye of almost any historic storm. The reputation of being chronic "troublemakers" was not an empty claim; many were involved in the risky business of revolutions, spying, fanaticism, and common criminality. To mention just a few: Tomas de Torquemada, Head of the Spanish Inquisition, and son of a converted Jewish mother, was responsible for burning many thousands of Jews and "witches" alive; Evno Azef, a provocateur and police agent, played a key role in the subversive underground in Russia in the turbulent beginning of the twentieth century. A decade later, in an attempt to undermine the Russian monarchy, another Jew, Alexander Parvus, a corrupt international manipulator, financed the Russian revolution of 1917 by channeling German money to the Bolsheviks during the First World War. His friend, Leon (Lev) Trotsky, probably the most talented revolutionary ever, built the Red Army and successfully managed the ruthless military campaign of the Bolsheviks during the Civil War. In 1918, a disturbed and almost blind Jewish woman, Fanny Kaplan, attempted to assassinate Vladimir Lenin (himself appearing to have had a Jewish grandparent). The wounded Lenin never fully recovered, and inter-Kremlin fighting for power ensued, which ended up with Stalin's dictatorship. The traditional Jewish preparedness of embracing social changes, reforms, and revolutions did not know any bounds, as the extraordinary life of Joe Slovo illustrates. He was the main organizer of the armed struggle against South-African apartheid and was born in 1926 into a Jewish-Lithuanian family, who, for mysterious reasons, migrated as far as South Africa when he was eight. The

NKVD (Soviet Secret Service) general Alexander Orlov (Lev Feldbin) directed political and military events of the Spanish Civil War in the thirties on behalf of the Soviet Intelligence. It is well-known that Jews constituted a significant portion of the upper echelon of the Soviet secret police at its early stage, but were arrested and shot later on. According to Pavel Sudoplatov, a shadowy chief of the subversion department of the NKVD, the absolute majority of Soviet spies in the Second World War was Jewish.

Jews also excelled in criminal activities. Along with Italian and Irish immigrants, they were at the roots of the American Mafia. In the thirties, the notorious Purple Gang dominated Detroit's underworld. A mobster, Bugsy Siegel, initiated the transformation of a dusty desert town of Las Vegas into a gambling empire. Foundations of Mafia affiliated financial mechanisms were set forth by Meyer Lansky. I should note in defense of Jewish gangsters that they did not make these activities a family business and took good care of education for their offspring, so the American Mafia lost its Jewish shade in the next generations. With the mass influx of immigrants from the previous Soviet Union, the FBI recorded new sprouts of the Jewish Mafia.

"Jews are News" is no empty phrase. Somehow they manage to stay on the very edge of current events, provide a media spin, and influence the agenda one way or another. In particular, Jews stand out in periods of great upheavals, like the Soviet revolution or the chaos in Germany in the aftermath of the First World War. These were Jews who cracked the hermetically closed Soviet system with their demand of mass emigration to Israel in the end of sixties, a dangerous undertaking, as anybody familiar with the Soviet Union would agree. Jews contributed to the dismantlement of the Soviet state as much as they did earlier to its formation. Many of the so-called "oligarchs", who made fortunes in the process of the recent wild privatization of the Soviet economy, are also Jewish. They rapidly adapted to the stream of events, when the huge and mighty country struggled in a rush to get rid of Communism. It seems that simple means, such as access to the inner circle of President Boris Yeltsin, including his Personal Security chief and his tennis coach, were key elements in gaining control over vital Russian assets.

The incredible fact of Jewish survival over so many centuries under hostile conditions, the intensity of their influence on the host nations, and the boldness of the Jewish spirituality are major reasons for anti-Semitism. People, who would declare their "choosiness" and, even worse, appear to support this statement by their very history, would look for troubles. It is not surprising that unusual characteristics of Jewish history gave rise to wide spectrum anti-Semitism, from the methodical extermination by the Nazis to its various mild brands. Jewish holy texts contained tough wording concerning the treatment deserved by gentiles, which should be seen in the light of animosity between the monotheistic Jews and pagans in ancient times. Similar statements may be found in texts adopted by other religions, especially in Islamic ones. Their true proportions come to light when compared, for example, to the deeds of the Spanish Inquisition or the Islamic conquest of Europe. These texts were recently used by Russian parliamentarians to file a formal request for prohibiting Judaism and the Jewish organizations as being racist.

For the most part of their history, the Jews were defenseless and there was no shortage of those who took pleasure in hitting the soft target. At the end of the fifteenth century the Inquisition Chief Torquemada staged what was probably the first show-trial in history, accusing eight Jews and converts of crucifying a Christian child. They were burned alive and their confession under torture was the only evidence. Since then rumors of ritual murders committed by Jews have circulated around the world for centuries, but not one case was proven. Characteristically, these accusations originated from the Catholic Inquisition, responsible for the well-documented ritual murder of many thousands of Jews and non-Jews in France, Spain and Portugal. Another wave of atrocities was associated with Bogdan Chmielnitcki, Ataman (chieftain) of the Ukrainian Cossacks, whose imposing statue dominates the center of Kiev. He waged a war against Poles in the middle of the seventeenth century; the main victims were Jews once again.

Some truly outstanding main-stream personalities were anti-Semites. The case of Henry Ford, a great industrialist, particularly stands out in this regard. Nazis affectionately referred to Henry as "our Heinrich"; Hitler was particularly touched, calling him "my inspiration". The reason for the Nazi delight was a series of articles known under the common title of "*The International Jew*", which Ford published in the twenties. He claimed, among other things, that Jews had plotted the First World War. One of the central arguments was that Jews themselves told him so; it was impossible to refute it as Ford had not bothered to identify even a single "deep throat".

We may be tempted to kick aside Ford's attitude as motivated by his commercial interests of a businessman in a permanent fight with Jewish competitors. Yet, one can pinpoint another brand of anti-Semitism: a spiritual type. Prominent gentiles, who helped to shape the civilized world, were anti-Semites, which is certainly something to think about. Among them such great Christian figures as novelist Fyodor Dostoevsky and theologian Martin Luther. Dostoevsky, still referring to Jews as a "great tribe", populated his books with Jewish characters of doubtful integrity. Luther systematically described Jews as "thieves and robbers" and initiated fierce anti-Jewish campaigns. Fagin, a career criminal, stars in Charles Dickens' "*Oliver Twist*", providing a marvelous opportunity for stereotyping the Jews; a moneylender Shylock in Shakespeare's "*The Merchant of Venice*" was a reflection of the Jewish occupation of usury. Thomas Eliot, probably the finest poet of the English-speaking world in the middle of the twentieth century, had major difficulties in avoiding anti-Jewish passages in his poetry; he won the Nobel Price in 1948. For Slavs, permanently depressed by what they see as the Western superior rationalism and inability of controlling their vast spaces, anti-Semitism was a daily routine, which "renders vodka stiffer and bread tastier", as mentioned by a Russian writer.

Hitler's paganism, combined with a myth of Aryan purity, led to the most monstrous anti-Semitic machinery. With the identity of Hitler's parental grandfather being the unresolved mystery, a theoretical possibility of having a Jewish ancestor was one of the irritating elements of his obsession. But a key factor was the prominence of Jewish figures during the period of social chaos in Germany at the end and in the aftermath of the First World War; destruction of European Jewry was a major behind-the-scenes motivation of the German attack on Poland and later on Russia.

Even Walter Schellenberg, Chief of the SS-intelligence, complained to his boss, Himmler, that the extermination of European Jewry "is worse then a crime, it is a folly". In his final hours, surrounded by the Red Army and buried deep in his underground bunker in the heart of devastated Germany, Hitler found nothing more urgent and important to deal with in his will than "International Jewry".

Presently, numerous Internet sites promote the same message: Jews are the universal source of evil on earth. Though most of them stick to conventional primitive propaganda, there are also "academic studies", saturated with falsified interpretations of Jewish sources; one of them claims to contain as many as two thousand pages. The notorious "*Protocols of the Elders of Zion*" is there for everybody to educate himself with. This central piece of conspiracy theory of world domination probably originated from the Tsarist police in a futile attempt to block the up-coming Russian revolution. This meme is far from being dead and, in fact, enjoys wide-spread support these days. In the wake of the terror attack of September 11, 2001, media openly discussed a possible Jewish involvement behind the scenes. The American invasion of Iraq was obviously a Jewish plot, aiming to strengthen Israel, as was the American drive for promoting democracy in the Muslim world. And the most recent crime is globalization, which results from the conspiracy of international corporations led by Jewish bankers.

A few years ago, Mohamed Mahathir, Malaysian's prime-minister of two decades and widely accredited for the modernization of his country, received loud applause by Muslim leaders when he proclaimed that Jews rule the world, nothing less. Trying to be fair, he went on by dropping a little bit of rationalism: "They survived two thousand years of pogroms, not by hitting back but by thinking....They invented socialism, communism, human rights and democracy, so that persecuting them would appear to be wrong, so that they can enjoy equal rights with others". Recently, Iran's President Mahmoud Ahmadinejad, leader of a major nation, openly called for wiping Israel off the map. Since Hitler no well-known politician has made statements of this sort.

Perhaps one may take comfort in the fact that Napoleon Bonaparte and Winston Churchill were admirers of the Jews. It was Napoleon who, with his series of decrees, played a key role in the emancipation of Jews in Europe after the Dark Ages with far-reaching consequences for the Jews and perhaps, for the entire world, as might be seen from the above. He even thought of recreating a Jewish state in Palestine and thus was among first Zionists. And this is what Churchill wrote in 1920: "Some people like Jews and some do not; but no thoughtful man can doubt the fact that they are beyond all questions the most formidable and the most remarkable race which has ever appeared in the world". I would make one more quote, of Mark Twain: "The Egyptian, The Babylonian, and the Persian rose, filled the planet with sound and splendor, then…passed away. The Greek and the Roman followed. The Jew saw them all, beat them all, and is now what he always was, exhibiting no decadence, no infirmities of age, no weakening of his parts….All things are mortal but the Jew, all forces pass, but he remains. What is the secret of his immortality?".

The obsession with Jews could take curious forms: the American mathematician John Nash, Nobel Prize winner, hero of the book "*A Beautiful Mind*", born in West Virginia to a Christian family, was hallucinating about Hebrew texts and Birobidzhan, the Jewish Autonomic Region in the Russian Far East near the border with China. He could have been influenced by the well-known Jewish contributions to mathematics. Still, the fixation on Birobidzhan, instead of, say, Brookline nearby, remains a mystery. In 1930, the British-Canadian author and artist Wyndham Lewis wrote a book intriguingly entitled "*The Jews: are They Human?*" But it was Nancy Yos, a recent convert, who has expressed the Jewish singularity in the most charming way: "I have found after all the books, cogitation, and self-absorption, a people without whom life would be intolerable".

Given the puzzling fact of this unique Jewish distinctiveness, for better or worse, it is not surprising that, over the centuries, this people attracted the attention of theologians, historians, sociologists, and philosophers genuinely interested in understanding the phenomenon. In particular, a critical and ample account of the Jewish involvement in Russian events over

the period of two centuries was recently written by Alexander Solzhenitsyn.

How was it possible for such a tiny group of people to make such a
decisive impact on human history? Was this wonder-story, which contained both the dazzling glory and the devastating tragedy, a result of
Divine intervention? According to the Jews, who point to the Covenant, it
is. But is it? This would absolutely contradict the widely accepted theories
claiming that the world just evolves in a random fashion without any long-
term plan. So, perhaps this is merely a "self-fulfilling prophecy", when a
whole ethnic group tries to prove the existence of such a plan in the effort
of cosmic proportions? Once again, the Jews are in the focus of a dispute.

The Covenant and its Breach

Paul Johnson comments that "the Jews were above all historians, and the
Bible is essentially a historical work from start to finish". Though there is
still considerable controversy about the historical validity of the Bible, the
prevailing opinion is that some of its chapters do have a factual basis, in
particular, those concerned with the conquest of Canaan and subsequent
events, while earlier accounts are mostly symbolic in nature. In recent
years, archeological discoveries have provided new circumstantial evidence
for Biblical narratives being more than mere stories.

Abraham, who was apparently a chieftain of the *Habiru* nomadic tribe,
moved with his people to Canaan from Mesopotamia, following God's
instructions, and become the first Jewish Patriarch. The Bible seems to
provide us with the first recorded real-estate deal, which took place around
2,000 B.C.E. in Hebron, now on the West Bank: Abraham purchased a
plot of land from a dignitary called Ephron for four hundred shekels. At
the beginning of the business transaction, Abraham made the following
striking confession: "I am a stranger and sojourner with you", which was
to become a hallmark of Jewish identity. Given this statement, can there
be any doubt that Abraham was Jewish?

Habiru people, scholars suggest, served as government employees, mer-
cenaries, merchants or tinkers, and are thought of as ancestors of what we

call the ancient Israelites. The book of Genesis describes three waves of settlements of Abraham and his immediate descendents in Canaan. The first one was associated with Hebron, as mentioned in the above, the second with Abraham's grandson Jacob, who settled in Shechem, presently Nablus on the West Bank. During the famine, Jacob's sons moved to Egypt and, when their descendents returned to Canaan, it was the third major wave of settlement. Jacob led a group of seventy men to Egypt. The Biblical tradition points to Jacob as the father of the twelve Hebrew tribes: *Reuben, Simeon (Levi), Judah, Issachar, Zebulun, Benjamin, Dan, Naphtali, Gad, Asher, Ephraim*, and *Manasseh*. When Israelites returned to Canaan four hundred thirty years later, in the event known as the Exodus, they numbered around six hundred thousand men. Demographers think these figures are reasonable, given the average life span of forty years and six children per household. It seems that Jacob was renamed Israel in order to mark the birth of a new nation. The term "Israel" has a variety of meanings, some of them mutually exclusive: he who fights for God, whom God rules, he whom God fights, and even he who fights God. This multiplicity is yet another illustration of the fact that almost everything that touches on a Jewish subject becomes controversial.

Though the stay in Egypt for many generations and the Exodus from there and the subsequent wandering in the Sinai Peninsula involved only a part of the Israelites, (with the other part still in Canaan) it was a critical phase in history of the nation; the all-mighty God they worshipped had delivered them from bondage and led them to the Promised Land, defeating the then only superpower on earth. In return, they were to meet God's expectations. They finally became the Chosen People for better or worse.

No other event seems to have molded the Jewish national character as decisively as the Exodus, probably the first successful revolt of slaves in history. On this occasion, God took care to remind the Jews that their freedom would not come free of charge and they would have to comply with the Covenant; God did this with a powerful, almost poetic language: "Ye have seen what I did to the Egyptians, and how I bare you on eagles' wings and brought you unto myself. Now therefore, if ye will obey My voice in deed, and keep My covenant, then ye shall be a peculiar treasure unto Me above all people". Thus, besides the natural motivation of physical survival, there was an explicit component of spirituality behind the Exodus. Historians estimate that the Exodus or a similar event occurred in the thirteenth century B.C.E., though many details remain vague. Already in those days, the Israelites had thought of themselves as a distinct nation bearing special responsibilities as dictated by the Covenant.

If Abraham was the biological father, Moses, who led the revolt and Exodus, was the spiritual father of the nation. Paul Johnson comments on Moses, stating that "mankind does not invariably progress by imperceptible steps but sometimes takes a giant leap, often under dynamic propulsion of a solitary, outsized personality". The Bible describes miracles performed by Moses in an effort to convince the Pharaoh "to let my people go"; indeed, these were to reach a specific outcome, not only proving Moses' capabilities as a prophet. Moses' legal and religious heritage constitutes the core of Jewish memes. Though the Bible sets Moses first of all as a prophet and lawgiver, it also expounds on his human failings. Characteristically, because of his sins, Moses was not allowed to enter the Promised Land, and was permitted only to take a look at it. He was the most influential personality of the ancient world until another Jew, Jesus, appeared on the scene of history.

After the conquest of Canaan under the leadership of Joshua, the chosen people were apparently shocked to find out that there was much to learn from the Canaanites, in particular, in pottery. They established the southern state of Judah and the northern state of Israel, though they also fought each other. In one of the encounters with invading Philistines, a recruit, David, killed the huge Philistine strongman, Goliath, with a sling and thereby gave birth to the famous meme of David and Goliath, which we recall until today. By skilful political maneuvering and military leadership, David soon became King of Judah, and then of all Israel; his reign is generally considered by Jews as the Golden Age. David also made another historic step by establishing his capital in strategically situated Jerusalem. He brought the most valuable religious relic to the city, the Ark of the Covenant, a sort of wooden chest with two Mosaic tablets containing the Ten Commandments. The Ark was the only physical evidence for the special bond between God and *His* people. David did not build the Temple, wisely preferring to minimize the ceremonial side of Judaism; although, the Bible suggests that God prohibited the construction, because David, as a military commander, had spilled too much blood.

Recent excavations at the top of the City of David in Jerusalem, led by Eilat Mazar, have unearthed remnants of a monumental structure at least ten meters wide and thirty meters long, built with a great deal of engineering sophistication. Pottery found at the site may be dated to the twelfth and eleventh centuries B.C.E., which immediately predates David's reign. This suggests that the structure could be the palace David erected after capturing Jerusalem from the Jebusites. Another find was a bulla, a round small clay seal, inscribed in Hebrew with the name of a minister of King Zedekiah, explicitly mentioned in the Book of Jeremiah.

The ambitious Temple was built by David's heir, Solomon, though in fact the latter was more interested in trade and women than in religion. Solomon was well-known for his wealth, wisdom, and power. Estimates show that around 1,000 B.C.E., the time of Solomon's kingdom, approximately two million Jews lived in the Promised Land. After Solomon's death, the Kingdom disintegrated once again into the two small states, Judah in the south and Israel in the north, both of which were to become a prey for the emerging superpowers: first, the Assyrians and then, the Babylonians. Toward the end of the seventh century B.C.E, Assyrians totally destroyed the northern Kingdom and exiled its population, ten Israeli tribes, to Assyria. It seems that they assimilated and vanished from the history of the Israelites. Jerusalem fell in 597 B.C. to the Babylonians. Israelites were either slaughtered or forced into exile; in 587–6 Jerusalem was again besieged and demolished. The Temple was torn down and the Ark of the Covenant lost, marking the beginning of the Diaspora. To put it simply, the Israelites became the Jews. The popular belief was that God had punished his people for the failure to comply with clauses of the Covenant.

The exile lasted for about fifty years during which Jews, without a state of their own, became submerged in religious thought and self-condemnation. It seems that the Persian king, Cyrus the Great, a follower of Zoroaster, initiated the return, which took place in several waves, though many preferred to remain in the Diaspora. Jerusalem and the Temple were rebuilt but on a smaller scale. The written text of the Bible was finalized, more or less as we know it, in the period of 400–200 B.C.E; thus, the Jewish tradition of propagating their memes in hardcopy form goes back about two millennia. Poetry and music also flourished, but the tolerant Persian rule was to come to its end. Alexander of Macedon crippled the Persian Empire in 332 B.C.E. From 332 to 200 B.C.E. Jews were under the stiff control of the Ptolemies, then the Seleucids, and the Hellenic culture gained popularity among nobility and intellectuals. Greeks however were polytheists, worshipping various narrowly specialized gods. When the Syrian strongman, King Antiochus IV, tried to force Judeans to Hellenize, prohibiting circumcision under the death penalty, they revolted.

Five sons of Matthias Hasmon, led by Judah the Maccabee, organized a successful guerilla war against the Seleucids and their collaborators and in 168–6 B.C.E., forced them out of Jerusalem and its vicinities. In about two decades, the Jews recovered their independent state which survived for the coming one hundred fifteen years. In 63 B.C.E., an influential chief-minister, Antipater, apparently half-Jew, arranged the Roman Empire hegemony over Judaea, which became a Roman client state. His son, Herod, first guaranteed himself firm Roman backing and then engaged in outrageous cruelties against his people and his own family. Herod terrorized pious Jews and nobility; he literally exterminated the Hasmonean dynasty and established a police state. He also erected colossal civil structures, especially in Jerusalem and Caesarea, and sponsored spectacular charities all over the Roman Empire and, in particular, rescued the Olympic Games from decay. Herod, who had a vague Jewish identity, built the magnificent Second Temple, which was much larger and luxurious than Solomon's Temple. The size of its components is amazing even by modern standards. Some of the lower stones are still there and weigh nearly one hundred tons.

With the death of Herod the Great in 4 B.C.E., the Jewish statehood effectively ceased to exist; it was reinstated only with creation of the modern state of Israel in the middle of the twentieth century. During the

Herodian period, there were about eight million Jews in the world, more than two million of them in Judaea.

Provided that their essential interests were secured, the Romans usually tolerated local traditions, and rebellions were a rare event. Jews once again were an exception. It appears that no other minority fought this great empire so fiercely and so long. During the first two centuries, there was a chain of uprisings. Since the Roman Empire was under the cultural domination of Greeks, it was in fact the rebellion against Greek paganism; there was a great deal of tension between these two ancient people, who had different views of the world and God. Though Philo of Alexandria, a famous philosopher, himself a Hellenized Jew, tried to merge the Jewish imagination with the Greek interest in nature, the competition between the monotheistic Jews and the Greeks, with their great but pagan culture, was a major source of ancient anti-Semitism. When the Greeks later converted to Christianity, they brought this luggage with them.

Various Jewish factions fought not only the Romans but also each other, so the uprisings had hardly any chance of success and were crushed by the iron fist. The Temple was burnt out; people were slaughtered or sold as slaves. The supporting Western wall of the Temple Mount, known presently as the Wailing Wall, was the only structural element to survive the destruction of the Second Temple, which took place in 70 C.E. It had become the symbol of the religious and national bond between Jews and the Land of Israel.

About one thousand insurgents took refuge in the Massada fortress, spectacularly situated on the rocks overlooking the Dead Sea and the desert, but Romans got there too; rebels, except for two women and five children, committed suicide, setting forth Massada's meme, which thrives up to these days. There are historians questioning the very fact of suicide or its circumstances. Josephus Flavius, a Jewish historian, is the single source of what we think happened at Massada. Only parts of his description have been confirmed by archeological excavations. For about two millennia, Massada was associated with the firmness of Jewish spirit (or, alternatively, with the Jewish lunacy) and panoramic scenery.

Recently, it has become known in another context because of the famous date palm tree of Judea. This was highly praised in both, the Bible and Koran for its medicinal qualities, beauty and taste, but it vanished in the wake of the Crusades. These dates provide me with opportunity of departing for the moment from the chain of horrible events which took place in the Land of Israel in the aftermath of the rebellion. During Massada excavations in the seventies, several seeds were found in a storeroom. Radiocarbon analysis of Swiss experts showed that the seeds were 1990±50 years old. Presumably, they had been left over from dates consumed by the fortress' defenders. This is only half the story. The second and most astonishing part comes in the spring of 2005: Elaine Solowey, an American-Israeli biologist, managed to awake them from their dormancy and one of the seeds germinated. By the summer of 2005, the plant reached nearly 30cm; presently, one of its seven leaves is undergoing DNA testing aimed at discovering secrets of the splendid Judea dates. In a way, this is a miracle.

Now I have to return to the results of the anti-Roman rebellions. It is estimated that in the last uprising in 132 C.E., led by Shimon Bar Kochba, nearly half-a-million Jews died. It was cheaper to buy a Jewish slave than a horse. The Romans annihilated the Jewish community but the physical destruction was not enough: they renamed Judea as *Palaestina* to erase any Jewish affiliation with the Land of Israel. The Arabic word *Filastin* originates from this Latin name having its roots in the Indo-European pagan people, Philistines, who populated the southern coastal area and fought the Hebrews for centuries. Finally, to make it lethal for the Jewish soul, the Romans took care to set remnants of the Temple as a site for pagan worship.

At this tragic intersection of their history, the Jews displayed an extraordinary capability for survival. Without the Temple and a state of their own, they could not go on sacrificing lambs to their God, so they began to pray in the present sense of this word. This, in turn, required intensive studies of the Holy Scriptures and, as a result, scholars became the Jewish nobility. There was yet another reaction of cosmic proportions: a new religion was born, Christianity, a pure product of Jewish spirituality. To put it simply, it was the Jewish Christianity. It was the outgrowth of the Jewish notion of Messiah. At first, Christians were Jews, as well as Jesus himself and all the prophets. However, other nations jumped at the opportunity. The Greeks were among the first, again leaving the Jews as a minority. The key point of bitter antagonism between the two religions was the divinity of Jesus: for Christians he was the Messiah, man *and* God, which was obviously a heresy for the strictly monotheistic Jews. Agreeing on almost anything else, the two parties were unable to bridge this crucial difference.

Besides the fundamental principles, Rabbinic Judaism tried to dictate small details of the daily life and behavior to the follower, which the Torah did not contain. By tradition, along with the Torah, Moses was granted the Oral Law on the top of Mount Sinai, which provides complementary interpretations and procedures. The Oral Law was put down in written form around 200 C.E. by Rabbi Judah HaNasi.

The Dark Ages

The Jewish presence in Arabia goes back to the sixth century B.C.E., especially around Medina where numerous Jewish tribes had settled. When another great monotheistic religion, Islam, began its victorious path in the Arabic Peninsula, Jews were once again in the very focus of events. Mohammed, like Moses, never claimed a Divine origin and, pursuing the destruction of local paganism, accepted the Jewish God and adapted Jewish customs and beliefs to a habitat of Arabic deserts. Islam recognized all the prophets, including Jesus, according to its own interpretation. The exclusiveness of a piece of land in far away Canaan was replaced by the exclusiveness of Mecca, and the Hebrew language was naturally replaced by Arabic. There was also a basic claim that the two earlier religions deviated from the Covenant: the Christians by splitting the single all-mighty God and the Jews by disobeying God.

Soon, Christianity and Islam had developed their own dogmas and sects as well as political and military ambitions, which changed the course of history and created a completely different world. As for the Jews, they were about to start yet another journey as a defenseless minority abandoned to the mercy of a host nation; they could repeat Abraham's words: "I am a stranger and sojourner with you". They were destined to pose a social problem, to which a host nation would try to find a solution, often painfully touching on the Jewish body and soul.

When the Jews of Medina rejected Mohammed as the prophet, they were slaughtered. In general, Muslims were more tolerant than Europeans, for, after all, Jews had not crucified Mohammed; they had merely refused to adopt him. Jews were also useful as doctors, traders, craftsmen, counselors and, most important, tax payers.

There had been prosperous Jewish communities in Spain since the Roman period but under Christian rule they were persecuted, flogged, forced to convert, and executed. This produced a sort of underground Jew, the *marrano*. Among others, Diego Rivera, a famous Mexican painter and leftist activist of the first half of the twentieth century, and Fidel Castro, the Communist ruler of Cuba, had *marrano* ancestors. Jews, therefore, assisted in the Islamic conquest of Spain. Because of the subsequent inter-Muslim fighting and resulting pogroms, many fled to Africa and to territories under Christian control. Among these refugees was Moses ben Maimon, known also as Rambam, who later became a world-wide authority as doctor and philosopher.

During the period of the Roman Empire, there were already Jewish communities in Western Europe. In the Dark Ages they spread eastward, to Poland, the Ukraine and the Baltic. The Jews were primarily town-dwellers: merchants, craftsmen, and dealers. They were systematically discriminated against and pressured to convert to Christianity, but their communication skills and mobility greatly enhanced their social significance.

There was, however, the occupation which made them particularly notorious: usury. Ironically, pagans did not prohibit profitable money lending, Jews were the first to conditionally forbid it: "Unto a stranger thou mayest lend upon usury; but unto thy brother thou shalt not lend upon usury". In other words, Jews did forbid usury, but only when applied to Jews. Judging by the standards of those times, it was a mild form of discrimination, especially if compared with the discrimination to which the Jews themselves as a minority were subject. Nevertheless, this charge was to become a major item in the long list of Jewish sins and was even immortalized by Shakespeare in "*The Merchant of Venice*".

The Jews lost their statehood many generations ago. The nobility, government officials, and the military disappeared as social strata of the Jewish communities. Jews were dispersed all over the world and were left at the will of unpredictable hosts. Can the situation be more fatal? Still, they managed to retain their coherent identity, religion, language, almost total literacy and the dream of somehow returning to Jerusalem in the future. Scholars, doctors and philosophers, of whom Rambam was a most prominent example, had become the Jewish "nobility". It is difficult to overestimate the enormous importance Jews had begun to ascribe to science and knowledge in general. There was a well-developed system of study and learning, not limited to religious matters. Rabbis were supposed to be knowledgeable in both science and history and Jewish doctors gained especially prestigious reputations. Expertise in philosophy, theology, and science was passed from one generation to the next, like a genetic trait. Given the absolute taboo on sex among close relatives, one could get the impression that Jews knew something about genetics in those times. There was also an esoteric stream of white and black magic, numerology, and, most important, the *Kabbalah* which developed into a major mystic teaching.

The attitude towards Jews depended on place and time. Safety and prosperity could turn out a tragedy in a moment. Christian clerics developed a theory claiming that Jews had knew the truth about Christ, the Messiah and Son of God, from the beginning but they had concealed it on purpose; they were obviously Devil's followers. Common people, mostly illiterate and often starving, believed that Jews had tails as a result of intercourse between Devil and Eve. Physical attacks, initiated by nobles and priests and executed by serfs, were wide spread. In 1095, Pope Urban II declared the Crusades, which further incited anti-Jewish feelings. Crusaders committed massacres in various European countries on their way to the Holy Land and then in Palestine, to celebrate their arrival. The First Crusade alone resulted in the killing of nearly a quarter of the Jews in the Rhineland. In 1290, Jews were expelled from England and in 1394 from France.

Working in a research lab in the sixties, I suddenly found out that my Russian colleague, a Ph. D. in Mathematics and a nice fellow who shared my admiration for Brazilian soccer, sincerely believed that Jews habitually added Christian blood to their Passover flat bread, the *matzah*. This story had its roots in the twelfth century, when Jews of Norwich, England, were accused of the sadistic murder of a Christian boy, while reenacting Christ's death. Later, this was followed up by a claim that Jews mixed the Passover bread with Christian blood; in other words, Jews were a sort of vampire. From that time, accusations of ritual murder and blood libel were to pursue the Jews for centuries. Converts were involved in these accusations, which made them more plausible. It took centuries for the Catholic Church to rethink its attitude towards Jews. It was only in 1965, the papacy in Rome eventually issued a statement which cleansed the Jews of the collective guilt for the death of Jesus.

A new wave of pogroms followed when the Bubonic Plague killed nearly half of the population of Western Europe. Jews were kept responsible for spreading the epidemic. Several Jews confessed, under torture, to committing the crime and, once again, converts supported the charges. In addition to Christian fanaticism, the Jewish occupation of money lending and the Jewish "otherness", seen in traditions such as circumcision, contributed to an outbreak of atrocities.

The Crusades came to the end in the thirteenth century, but the break was short. At the end of the fifteenth century, the Spanish monarchs Ferdinand and Isabella announced the creation of an Inquisition which was, first and foremost, meant to seek and destroy the "pseudo-Jews".

Though converts were among the participants of anti-Semitic plots, this time they were the main victims: about thirteen thousand were condemned over a period of twelve years. Altogether, more than twenty thousand people of Jewish origin were killed, most of them burnt alive. The ferocious persecution spread to practically every corner of Spain, though the papacy in Rome objected to its scale. In 1492, as a "final solution", the Edict of Expulsion was signed prescribing every Jew to leave Spain or convert under the immediate penalty of death. Towards the end of the year, the ancient and vibrant Jewish community had ceased to exist. Jews also expelled from Vienna, Cologne, Milan and other European cities, migrated to Eastern Europe, Poland in particular, as well as Africa and back to the Arab countries.

From the fourteenth century it became customary to differentiate between two ethnic groups: Spanish or *Sephardi* Jews and German or *Ashkenazi* Jews. These communities developed their own dialects; the Sephardim spoke Ladino, the Ashkenazim spoke Yiddish. One of the first ghettos was built in Venice in 1515–6 with the purpose of protecting Christians from the corruptive Jewish influence. In 1632, there were about two thousand five hundred Jews in the ghetto out of the nearly one hundred thousand Venetians; and this invention then spread to other European cities. Jews were obliged to pay special taxes and wear a distinct sign, like a piece of yellow cloth on a hat. Ghettos however also served as shelters fostering cultural life and traditions. Jews were intensely involved in trade and crafts, and, in particular, in rapidly growing print shops. If taken captives during wars, Jews were again traded as slaves, especially by Malta-based Christian friars. This profitable business flourished for about three hundred years, and it took Napoleon to end it.

The rise of Protestantism in the sixteenth century intensified anti-Jewish feelings. The great reformer, Martin Luther, wrote a passionate anti-Semitic pamphlet claiming that "their synagogues should be set on fire, and whatever is left should be buried in dirt". He claimed that Jews, whom he called "poisonous envenomed worms", should be drafted into forced labor, and so forth. Luther also organized expulsion of Jews from German towns.

Psychologists point out that the very fact of resettlement encourages entrepreneurial spirit and the invention of new ways of doing things. Jews, the eternal migrants, proved the case. The emerging capitalistic economy enabled Jews, a persecuted minority, to engage in entrepreneurial activity under conditions of free competition. They promoted a view that money is just a commodity like land, grain or house; there was, therefore, nothing wrong in lending money, provided the interest was reasonable. In search for freedom and prosperity, Jews moved to the American continent and to Eastern Europe, as far as Russia, playing a key role in money transfer, trade, crafts and as middlemen in agriculture. By 1575, there were already nearly one hundred fifty thousand Jews in Poland. If the authorities tolerated them, it was only because they were wealth-producers. As such, Duke of Savoy even initiated Jewish settlements in Nice and Turin. About that time, Habsburg monarchs and Jews developed special ties based on mutual interests, which appear to have survived up to these days. On the other hand, the Russian Tsar Ivan the Terrible confronted them with the old dilemma: convert or die. At that time, Jews were formally prohibited from entering Russia. This decree was enforced until the late eighteenth century.

Tragedies and Hopes

During the Thirty Years War, 1618–48, Jews played a significant role in supplying goods for fighting armies and, in particular, delivering crops raised by Polish and Ukrainian peasants. The main beneficiaries were Polish landlords, but Jews, as middlemen, were perceived by the impoverished Ukrainian peasantry as the main oppressors; a mutiny was unavoidable. An additional irritating factor was the Jewish involvement in the production and distribution of alcohol. For marginal foreigners forbidden to own land, this was a way of surviving. It appeared that Jews first exploited peasants to squeeze maximum profits and then sold them vodka to drink away their wretchedness. Much later, one of the Russian writers, discussing the national thirst for alcohol, sarcastically noted in this regard that Siberian peasants, who never encountered a Jew, were as heavy drinkers as people in western Russia subjected to corruptive Jewish influence.

In 1648, Bogdan Chmielnitcki, an unknown Ukrainian aristocrat, the so-called Ataman, who was apparently motivated by a property rivalry with Polish nobles, conducted a bloody war of the Ukrainian Cossacks against the Polish rule and the Catholic Church. The first victims were, of course, Jews, the defenseless foreigners. By approximate account, nearly one hundred thousand Jews were slaughtered. These events are engraved in the Jewish national history as Chmielnitcki's catastrophe, though his personal role in these atrocities remains uncertain.

The migration back to the West, especially, to Holland, England and Germany, was a result of these massacres. Once again, Messianic ideas became popular and a Messiah had indeed appeared as Shabettai Zevi, born in 1626 in Smyrna, Turkey. His main mentor and guide was a young brilliant kabalist, known as Nathan of Gaza. Zevi was mentally unstable, according to various accounts he was incapable of sexual intercourse, so that his first two wives divorced him. He married again: his third wife was a pretty woman, though of doubtful reputation. It remained a mystery whether this affected his sexual performance, but it seemed to improve his chances as Messiah: knowledgeable sources pointed out that one of the Biblical prophets, Hosea, had married a whore. Jews were always good in spreading rumors; in this case they were so good that some European Jews sold their property and traveled to Palestine in anticipation of the coming Messiah. After wandering around and performing miracles here and there, Zevi eventually showed up in Constantinople. Modesty was not among his traits, by some accounts he entertained the thought of converting the sultan to Judaism. In Constantinople, he was arrested. When brought before the High Council, Zevi changed his mind and refused to declare himself Messiah. Given the familiar choice between conversion and death, he accepted Islam and became Aziz Mehmed Effendi. He was even assigned a generous pension; later, some of his followers in Poland converted to Christianity and supported accusations of the blood libel.

Despite enthusiasm about the coming of the Messiah and occupation with the Kabbalah, Jews did not abandon rational thinking, a tradition which went back to Rambam. Because of God's constant watch over their deeds and thoughts, as dictated by the Covenant, Jews developed an unprecedented capacity for self-criticism. Its roots were in the Bible, which was flooded with descriptions of their weaknesses, sins, and failures. The time was ripe for the Bible itself to come under scrutiny. Baruch (Benedict) Spinoza was born in Amsterdam in 1632 to Sephardic parents. After receiving a rabbinical education, he could not resist the classic Jewish temptation of intellectual rebellion and developed his own views about the essence of God and the origins of the Bible. He stressed that God exists as the unity and harmony of the universe, rejected the immortality of soul and insisted on scientific analysis of the Bible, just like other historic documents. For this heresy, Spinoza was excommunicated by Amsterdam's rabbis. Many claimed that he was in fact an atheist. He managed to make his living as a grinder of optical lenses. It was only after his death in 1677 that Spinoza was acknowledged as one of the greatest philosophers in the history of mankind.

Spinoza's critical rationalism could not interest Jews struggling to survive in poor Jewish settlements, the so-called *shtetels*, of Western Russia, Lithuania and Poland. The Ba'al Shem Tov born as Israel ben Eliezer in 1700 in Podolia, Ukraina, offered them a practical and inspirational approach to spirituality known as *Hasidism*, which was to fill the vacuum left by the evaporated Messiah, Shabettai Zevi. Shem Tov first earned a reputation as a successful healer and rabbinical proxy, possessing supernatural powers. He went on by introducing the notion of *zaddik*, a human who, though not a Messiah, possessed nevertheless superior spiritual qualities. These became mentors and guides of the new Hasidic movement. Shem Tov introduced a revolutionary way of praying which was, he insisted, a Divine act, to be accompanied by absolute annihilation of the personality and complete submission to the Torah, the very letters of which were Holy. His successor, Dov Baer, invoked the following powerful description: "When a man studies or prays, the word should be uttered with full strength, like the ejaculation of a drop of semen from his whole body, where his entire strength is present in that drop". The joy and passion implanted in Hasidic ceremonials were of particular appeal to impoverished Jews. On the other hand, Elijah ben Zalman Kramer, known as the *Gaon* (genius) *of Vilna* was a fierce opponent of Hasidism. He was an exceptional prodigy as a child and later became known as a scholar, especially in the field of mathematics, and religious authority. He claimed that the institution of zaddik led to the worship of a human being, the sinful idolatry, and that noisy Hasidic prayers and ecstasies were a harmful delusion. Nevertheless, Hasidism became an integral part of Judaism.

By the end of the seventeenth century, English Jews began to enjoy, at least in theory, equal rights. The situation in North America, desperately in need of colonists, was also improving. Jews settled in New York, Rhode

Island, Philadelphia and Delaware; they built houses, synagogues and even voted in elections. There, without the rigid restraints of royal and religious establishments, their energy and improvisation came heavily into play. Roots of American Jewry, which was destined to influence major historic events in the years to come, were laid. Towards the end of eighteenth century, legal restrictions, such as the ban on Jews attending universities and the obligatory yellow badge, were removed by Joseph II of Austria.

Nonetheless, with increasing secularization of the European culture, Jews were to meet a new challenge in the form of the main promoters of the Enlightenment, Voltaire and Diderot, who were profoundly anti-Semitic. Voltaire blatantly referred to Jews as "a totally ignorant nation who for many years has combined contemptible miserliness and the most revolting superstition with a violent hatred of all those nations which have tolerated them". Diderot was no better: "The Jews have always displayed contempt for the clearest dictates of morality and the law of nations". They were regarded as bitter opponents of human progress on the one hand and as subversive anarchists on the other, depending on one's position. This was, once again, the familiar dual perception of the Jews.

It took Napoleon to make the situation less abusive. In 1806, he issued an order convening an Assembly of Jewish Notables and then declared the Jews as "French citizens of the Mosaic faith". Napoleon went on by convening the Sanhedrin, a meeting of religious experts, to advise the Assembly on issues of the Torah. This later backfired when it triggered the infamous conspiracy theory and eventually led to the "*Protocols of the Elders of Zion*". Good intentions do not necessarily bring about good results. It seems that Napoleon's first encounter with a Jewish community took place during his Italian campaign in 1797. He closed ghettos and issued a decree allowing the Jews to reside wherever they wanted, as well as to freely practice their religion. During his Palestinian campaign in 1799, Napoleon was prepared to declare a Jewish state there. Later in 1816, already in exile, the Great Little Corsican elaborated his special attitude towards the Jews in the following way: "My primary desire was to liberate the Jews and make them full citizens. I wanted to confer upon them all the legal rights of equality, liberty and fraternity as was enjoyed by the Catholics and Protestants. It is my wish that the Jews be treated like brothers as if we were all part of Judaism. As an added benefit, I thought that this would bring to France many riches because the Jews are numerous and they would come in large numbers to our country where they would enjoy more privileges than in any other nation. Without the events of 1814, most of the Jews of Europe would have come to France where equality, fraternity and liberty awaited them and where they could serve the country like everyone else." By any standards, this was extremely unusual for those times. It was no surprise that the Jews regarded Napoleon as a Messiah.

The liberal spirit of the European Enlightenment and technological advances had a major effect on European Jewry, the Ashkenazim. With legal restrictions lifted, they deepened their participation in trade, banking, industry and free-lance occupations. Improved living conditions led to their population growth.

Emancipation and Dead End

The Industrial Revolution of the nineteenth century was an opportunity European Jews could not miss. Their improvisation, mobility, and pragmatism had accelerated the development of capitalism. The Rothschilds and other Jewish bankers expanded international operations. Still, conversion was seen by many as the only way to achieve equality. Benjamin Disraeli, baptized as a teenager, was an example of the rewards baptism could offer. He was a brilliant debater and novelist. He also had a reputation as a dandy and was known for his extravagant dress. He became England's first and only Jewish prime-minister and the founder of the Conservative Party. He brought the Suez Canal and India under control of the British Empire. To him, Christianity was the "completed Judaism" and he blamed Jews for ignoring this. Disraeli was one of the early Zionists and was said to have muttered in Hebrew when he died in 1881. He viewed Israel as the heart of human body and was proud of his Jewish ancestry, which, in his words, "had developed a high civilization at a time when the inhabitants of England were going half naked and eating acorns in the woods". This sort of argumentation would later reemerge from time to time in confrontations between Jews and gentiles. Fritz Houtermanns, a German physicist, who managed to endure interrogations of both, the Soviet secret police NKVD and Gestapo, and was "only" one quarter-Jewish, expressed the same idea in his own way. While engaged in such a dispute, he commented: "When your ancestors were still living in the trees, mine were already forging cheques!".

Karl Marx was baptized when a boy in 1824 and was of another sort. Marx's parents came from lines of famous rabbis and scholars, which did not prevent his father from converting, a move which advanced his career as a lawyer. Marx, whose theory of class struggle had changed the world, was considered one of the most influential social thinkers to emerge in the nineteenth century. It took the horrifying crimes of the Soviets, committed decades after his death (though on his behalf but obviously without his approval), to discredit his revolutionary doctrines. Today, his economic analysis of capitalism is considered deficient. Marx was explicitly anti-Jewish: "Money is the jealous God of Israel, besides which no other god may exist...The god of the Jews has been secularized and has become the god of this world". His ample "*Capital*" contained the following comment: "The capitalist knows that all commodities, however scurvy they may look, or however badly they may smell, are in faith and in truth money, inwardly circumcised Jews". Another outstanding convert, Heinrich (Chaim) Heine, a great German poet, was also experiencing periodic attacks of self-hate. Both of these baptized Jews could turn, as a routine, to primitive anti-Jewish clichés in their private correspondence. Nevertheless, they became, especially the former, favorite stars of the rapidly growing Jewish intelligentsia, which was mostly secularized and leftist and which produced a group of socialistic leaders and activists. The latter fact was exploited in the years to come by anti-Semitic propaganda, in particular, by the Nazis, to display the Jews as conspirators and troublemakers.

German Jews were a minority never exceeding one percent of population. Amos Elon writes in his recent book that "one wonders how so small a presence could have triggered, even indirectly, such vast enmity". The first anti-Jewish Congress gathered as early as in 1882 at Dresden and was followed by meetings at Kassel in 1886 and at Bochum in 1889. German anti-Semitism was always of a wide spectrum and encompassed all social strata, from folks to church, to business, to nobility. By the end of nineteenth century, there appeared a new anti-Semitic strain in the form of neo-paganism, which was to be felt in the years to come. Paul de Lagarde, a linguist, promoted the idea that Christianity was merely a Jewish chimera and called for a specifically German religion based on the purity of German people as a Master Race. Jews were "vermin" to be exterminated "as quickly and thoroughly as possible". Richard Wagner, a great composer, followed his steps, but it took another pagan, Adolf Hitler, to implement this plan several decades later.

German Jewry, despite the intense anti-Semitism or perhaps because of it, produced an astonishing row of industrialists, doctors, scientists, musicians, and social thinkers, among them Moses Mendelssohn, Albert Einstein, Sigmund Freud and Gustav Mahler. Jews felt that Germany was their home; after all, the both nations shared great respect for professionalism, intellect, science, and art, especially music. A guidebook to the city of Berlin comments that "the history of literature in Berlin begins on an autumn day in 1793 when a fourteen-year-old Talmudic student named Mendelssohn entered the city through the gate reserved for Jews and cattle". Until 1933, Germany has won about thirty percent of the Nobel Prizes, of which Jews were a third and in medicine a half. They also engaged, like Germans, in sports, winning sixteen Olympic medals for Germany during the first two decades after the revival of the games. Yiddish, a language of European Jews, had no words for military terms; yet, as noted by Paul Johnson, German Jews were awarded more than thirty thousand Iron Crosses in the First World War. Curiously, Jewish students had a reputation of being skillful and dangerous duelists.

Still, the feeling of alienation was always there. The dead-end perception was best described by the writer, Jacob Wassermann: "Vain to seek obscurity. They say: the coward, he is creeping into hiding, driven by his evil conscience. Vain to go among them and offer them one's hand. They say: why does he take such liberties with his Jewish pushfulness? Vain to keep faith with them as a comrade-in-arms or a fellow citizen. They say: he is a Proteus, he can assume any shape or form. Vain to help them strip off the chains of slavery. They say: no doubt he found it profitable."

During the nineteenth century, there was a dramatic shift in the demography of the Jewish people. Due to low standards of living in Asia and Africa, the number of Sephardim increased only slightly, approaching about seven hundred fifty thousand in 1880. By that time, they constituted nearly ten percent of World Jewry. European Jews, Ashkenazim, benefited from social and technological changes and their number leapt to seven million. Jewish families were stable; infant mortality was lower and the average life span was longer than that of gentiles, especially in Eastern Europe. Marriages between teenagers, (boys of fifteen with girls of fourteen), were common. By 1914, the total population had increased to thirteen million, almost all of them city dwellers. Due to a dynamic European environment, Ashkenazim were mobile, inventive and, in many instances, rebellious. That is why the explosion in the Ashkenazi population, which occurred towards the end of nineteenth century, was destined to influence the dramatic historical events in the years to come.

Russia is an immense and resourceful country; but it always had difficulties controlling its vast spaces, volatile climate, and heterogeneous population. A solution was found in the absolute power of the Tsar and then of Stalin. Serfdom was abolished only in 1861, not as the result of popular revolution but by Tsarist decrees. Periodically, governmental efforts were made to modernize the country and narrow the disparity between Russian intelligentsia, well-known of its great scientific traditions and classic literature, and the peasants, the so-called *muzhiks*, which led to only minor results. It should be noted that Jews did not practice slavery and had rebelled against their bondage around two millennia earlier. This illustrates the enormous gap in the backgrounds of these two peoples.

The Tsarist regime always viewed Jews as unacceptable foreigners and treated them much harsher than the rest of the population. Western powers had learnt "to live with Jews", milking them most of the time and occasionally persecuting them. The Russian governments had seen to it that the Jews would constantly be oppressed, as a method. There was no rational attempt or simply desire to incorporate them as an integral part of the Empire.

The "Jewish question" became particularly acute in 1793, when Polish territories with a sizable Jewish population were occupied. The government moved quickly to confine Jews to the so-called Pale of Settlement, which in its final form included the western provinces from the Black Sea to the Baltic. A special police permit was needed to leave the Pale. Nicolas I issued the *Cantonist Decrees* which *conscripted all Jewish males from twelve to twenty-five*. The Jewish educational system was effectively destroyed, Jews were categorized as the useful and the useless and discriminating legislation was put in place, including restriction quotas at Russian universities. Discrimination was enforced even in the military where Jews were excluded from officer status or from serving in the navy.

With few exceptions, Jews were desperately poor and were harassed on a daily basis by police, church, and peasants. A series of pogroms began in1871 in Odessa, provoked by Greek merchants, and then spread over Western Russia with the authorities turning a blind eye to or even bolstering the violence. An example is the pogroms of 1881 initiated by the Minister of the Interior, Ignatiev, in the wake of the assassination of Alexander II by the Pole, Ignacy Hryniewiecki. The years 1905–6 were especially bloody when mob massacred hundreds of Jews in Kishinev, Odessa and Bialystok. In the latter case, the police and army joined in the pogrom. Time and again, Jews were exploited by the authorities as scapegoats in an effort to "save Mother Russia" from upcoming upheavals. In a way, it was a small-scale rehearsal of the Holocaust, which took place several decades later in Europe under the Nazis.

The encounter of the two peoples, Russians and Jews, which lasted for roughly two hundred years, was highly problematic from the very beginning. It was the will of history or just bad luck, for the ancient tribe to find itself at the mercy of the mighty Slavic nation lost in its immense spaces. For the Russians, on the other hand, the very presence of the poor and defenseless but ambitious and restless non-natives, almost aliens, was a major source of irritation.

These tragic events had far-reaching consequences. First, they triggered a flight of Jews from Russia and Eastern Europe westwards, mainly to the United States, and thereby helped form the influential American Jewry. Second, they planted seeds of Jewish revenge that would develop through their mass participation in Russian subversive movements. Despite the warning of Zionists, Jewish involvement in revolutionary movements and the subsequent Civil War was so extensive that it bordered an invasion. The Zionist leader, Zeev Zhabotinsky, commented that "when Jewish masses rushed to do Russian politics, nothing good followed...". However, in a few years, with the conquest of power by Stalin and the expulsion of Leon Trotsky, who was considered as a main force behind the Bolsheviks' victory, there was no genuine Jewish influence on the character of the Soviet Communism, which was rapidly becoming more and more anti-Semitic.

In 1953, the Soviets officially announced the "Doctors' Plot" of exterminating Soviet leaders, including Stalin, to a stunned world. Almost all the arrested "killers" were Jewish physicians from the Kremlin's hospital, who "confessed" to spying and being Zionist agents. A poisonous campaign against "Zionists and Cosmopolites" was unleashed that spread throughout the vast country. Knowing Stalin's habits very well, Jews were preparing themselves for mass deportation to Siberia. Fortunately, Stalin soon suffered a stroke and died (no Jewish physicians were around!) and the surviving prisoners released.

Because the Soviet Union provided the Arabs with costly military, economic and political support, the swift Israeli victory in the Six Day War of 1967 was widely perceived as a humiliating defeat. The tiny country dared to resist not only its much larger neighbors but also challenged one of the two superpowers. When Nikita Khrushchev and after him Leonid Brezhnev tried to promote their liberalization policy, Soviet Jews were among the first to realize the uniqueness of the moment. It was a rare opportunity for dismantling the huge, suppressive, anti-Semitic empire. It is true that the Soviet Union experienced major economic difficulties, but it was the mass Jewish emigration as well as the Solidarity movement in Poland, which began to push it overboard.

American Jewry, on the other hand, was from the very beginning accepted as an integral part of the new nation from both legal and religious points of view; in 1790, George Washington wrote to the Jewish Community in Newport, Rhode Island, that "the United States gives bigotry no sanction, to persecution, no assistance." Jews became an essential component of the American business world, especially in New York, though they settled all over the country. They even resorted to arms to defend themselves, which would hardly have been thinkable in the Old World in those times. A recorded incident, which involved a Savannah Jew, Philip Munis, and a member of the Georgia legislature James Stark, took place in 1832. The latter publicly called Munis "a damned Jew...who ought to be pissed upon". After negotiations over apology versus duel, Munis shot Stark dead in a bar when the abuser drew his pistol. Munis was tried and acquitted.

During the Civil War there were some seven thousand Jews fighting for the North and three thousand for the South. Judah Benjamin was elected as Louisiana's senator in 1853 and served in this capacity until 1861; following these, he became a member of Confederate President Jefferson Davis' cabinet, as attorney general, then as Secretary of War, and finally, as Secretary of State. This did not imply the absence of anti-Jewish feelings or their manifestations. The situation was not always rosy: General Grant issued the notorious Order No. 11, expelling the "Jews as a class" from the states of Mississippi, Kentucky, and Tennessee, which was later annulled by President Abraham Lincoln in 1863. There were street hooliganism and discrimination by private clubs, hotels, and schools against Jews. The Ku Klux Klan was also very active in the South.

Traditionally, Jews were good in new areas; they founded the National Labor Movement, huge department stores, publishing houses, movie industries and the leading newspapers, *The New York Times* and *The New York Post*. It was a young Jewish poetess, Emma Lasarus, who wrote the famous sonnet inspired by the raising of the Statue of Liberty:

> *Give me your tired, your poor,*
> *Your huddled masses yearning to breathe free,*

The wretched refuse of your teeming shore.
Send these, the homeless, tempest-tos't to me.

By the beginning of the twentieth century, Jews were arriving at Ellis Island in New York at the rate of about eighty thousand a year. The heart of American Jewry was the Lower East Side of New York; where, by 1910, half-a-million impoverished Jews were tightly packed. Jewish clothing firms, New York's main industry, employed more than three hundred thousand people, mainly Jews, working day and night. In New York, Jews made up almost thirty percent of the population and represented the largest ethnic group.

Criminal history during those times is also flooded with Jewish names. Jews participated in illegal liquor trade and big business crime, including gambling, white slavery and murders. Many notorious gangsters were Jewish. For poor desperate immigrants, it was a way of getting rich; this however was not passed down to progeny as a family trait. By 1914, nearly two million had emigrated to the New World, mainly from Russia and Eastern Europe, with five and half million still in Russia and two and half million in the Austrian Empire. In 1920, already 1,640,000 Jews were living in New York and four and half million in the States. The creation of a sizable American Jewish population was a crucial factor in altering the character of Jewish influence in the world.

The liberal American atmosphere promoted a further split in Judaism, especially from the 1960s. The Reform movement, popular among well-to-do German Jews, stressed education and rationality and set aside traditional limitations regarding diet, dress, and religious purity. It saw God mainly as an abstraction and removed as many restrictions as possible from religious life. It believed in equality of women, including female rabbis and cantors, mixed seating in synagogues, the participation of gays and lesbians in religious services. There are presently almost one thousand Reform congregations, which unite nearly a million and a half Jews. For Orthodox Jews, this was a sinful breach of the Covenant, which once again could bring about God's reprisals. They kept adhered to the normative Orthodox Judaism, as it was formulated during the centuries of Diaspora. Both the Written and Oral Torah were of Divine origin, and represented the word of God in its literal sense; Rambam's "*Thirteen Principles of Faith*" was considered a core document of Orthodox Judaism. The third branch, Conservative Judaism, tried to bridge the two extreme approaches. Conservative Jews stress the importance of traditions: circumcision, strict procedures for marriage or divorce, a kosher diet, and recognition of Jewish lineage through matrilineal descent only; however, they attach lesser importance to the literal formulations of the Holy Scriptures. Even so, the Jewish appetite for diversity was not satisfied. The three main streams not only fought each other but, with time, further split into various sub-streams. Orthodox Jews were especially restless, branching into ethnic sects, some of them ferociously anti-Zionist. There was also a fourth stream: assimilation and denial of Jewish identity. The typical representatives of this trend were Presidential adviser, Bernard Baruch, who was sometimes referred to as "the Acting President of the United States", and news commentator, Walter Lippmann.

Traditionally, Jews participated in American politics, representing a wide spectrum of positions, from left-wing propagandists of various shades to right-oriented conservatives. The prominent linguist Noam Chomsky, son of immigrants from Russia, described himself as a "libertarian socialist". Recently, visiting the headquarters of Hezbollah, the militant Lebanese group, which initiated suicidal bombing, he praised its struggle against Israel and the United States. On the other hand, influential neo-conservatives, such as Paul Wolfowitz, President of the World Bank, supported the hawkish foreign policy and restrictions on social spending.

Jaws of Hydra

In the twenties, anti-Jewish sentiments were on the rise in Europe and in the States due to the catastrophic consequences of the First World War and the economic crisis. Jews, prominent in nearly every possible field, were publicly blamed for causing the war. Henry Ford promoted these accusations, quoting the *Protocols of the Elders of Zion* on every occasion. In Germany, devastated by the war, Jews were held responsible for everything: Jewish financiers had plotted the war, Jewish politicians had corrupted the home front and stabbed the heroic army in the back, and Jews had evaded the military service and had profited from the German disaster.

By the very beginning of the thirties, Stalin was already firmly in power in Russia and pursued his own agenda of total domination of the huge, disordered but resourceful country by means of indiscriminate terror. He also suppressed anything genuinely Jewish. But the perception of the Soviet Communism as a Jewish enterprise in the frameworks of Jewish control of the world was very much alive and was another crucial factor in the rise of Nazism.

Crucial historic events rarely result from the actions of a single person. Nevertheless, Nazism was, from its beginning to its end, Hitler's creation. It is also true, that he enjoyed the sincere, if not passionate, cooperation of Germans and Austrians, without which history of the mankind would look much better. Hitler had no serious education whatsoever, but was gifted with an understanding of human psychology, great political pragmatism, and exceptional willpower. Most of all, he had the highest ambitions and had neither human warmth nor compassion. This was indeed an explosive mixture in itself. This greatest promoter of purity of the Master Race also suffered from a set of illnesses and consumed risky drugs on a daily basis. This is described in a recent book by Mike Haskins: "Every morning Hitler's physician, Dr Theo Morell, would give the Führer a "vitamin shot". Before receiving this boost Hitler was said to be extremely lethargic. Afterwards, as Himmler noted, he perked up a treat and became alert, active and ready to go about his business....Adolph's "vitamin shots" were alternated with tablets including Pervitin, which was a commercial brand of methamphetamine. Dr Morell is said to have administered at least ninety two different drugs to the Führer during World War II.".

Displaying the Jews as the fundamental source of evil on earth served as a vehicle for Hitler's drive to power. At the end of the thirties, there was a short period of time when, to calm international protests, the Nazis assisted the Jewish emigration to Palestine and also played with a plan of shipping the Jews to Madagascar, but Hitler quickly became worried about a "new power base for world Jewry" and the policy was switched to physical elimination. There is no doubt that already in the twenties Hitler had made up his mind regarding extermination of Jews as a main goal of his life. In 1919, while serving in the German army as a volunteer, he was asked by an officer for his thoughts on Jews. He replied pedantically in writing that "Jew power is the power of the money, which multiplies in his hands effortlessly and endlessly through interest, and with which he imposes a yoke upon the nation that is the more pernicious in that its glitter disguises its ultimately tragic consequences....purely emotional antiSemitism finds its final expression in the form of pogroms. Rational antiSemitism, by contrast, must lead to a systematic and legal struggle against, and eradication of, the privileges the Jews enjoy over the other foreigners living among us (Alien Laws). Its final objective, however, must be the total removal of all Jews from our midst".

Nearly twenty six years later, Hitler, exhausted and strained, was dictating his final will inside his Berlin's bunker bombarded by the victorious Red Army. He found nothing more relevant and urgent to deal with than to blame the Jews for the catastrophe. The peace offer he had made just before the start of the war "...was only rejected because the ruling clique in England wanted war, partly for commercial reasons and partly because it was influenced by the propaganda put out by international Jewry.... I have left no one in doubt that if the people of Europe are once more treated as mere blocks of shares in the hands of these international money and finance conspirators, then the sole responsibility for the massacre must be borne by the true culprits: the Jews.". Thus, Hitler's political involvement began and ended with Jews.

In addition to the political gains following from his widely publicized anti-Semitism, Hitler obviously had his personal, special reasons for his maniacal fixation on Jews. In his own way, Hitler was a calculating, rational person and this deeply emotional obsession could hardly be explained. There were rumors, especially spread by the post-war Soviet propaganda and disillusioned Nazis, that he was one-quarter Jewish, as his paternal grandmother supposedly got pregnant while serving a Jewish family in Graz, Austria. Historians argue that Jews were expelled from this city back in the fifteenth century and were not allowed to return until the 1860s, well after the alleged pregnancy. It remains, however, a theoretical option for Hitler, as well as for anybody else. After all, one may always doubt the real identity of one's father, needless to say that of one's grandfather. (That is why the Jewish tradition of specifying a person's religious lineage as maternal is well founded.)

As any great dictator, Hitler was also a great *director*, staging grandiose mass shows with explicitly masculine overtones, such as the Party rally in Nuremberg; he also took pleasure in personally supervising designs of fascist visual symbols and uniforms, all of them excessively theatric. In a sense, the Third Reich was a mixture of total sophisticated violence and theatre. This could have resulted from his political or artistic interests but may also have pointed to a troubled sexual identity. Hitler's relations with lovers remain vague, including his long-time intimate companionship with Eva Braun; his secretary, Traudle Junge, elaborated: "I did not think the relationship with Eva was very erotic. I do not think he was prepared to let himself go…which is important in erotic matters".

There was a theory that Hitler contracted syphilis from a Jewish prostitute or via a Jewish pimp during his years in Vienna as a vagabond, or, at least, had a traumatic sexual encounter involving Jews. Once again, there is no firm validation, though Jewish prostitutes or pimps were of course no rarity in those times (or at present). Hitler stressed time and again that not only Jewish financiers on the West and Jewish Bolsheviks on the East posed a threat, but that mortal danger was imminent from sexual contacts with Jews, the polluters of the pure Aryan genetic pool. Characteristically, he referred to syphilis as a Jewish disease and dealt with it at length in his "*Mein Kampf.*" This focus on syphilis in the specific Jewish context was highly unusual, even for the most vicious anti-Semites, and hinted at personal needs for doing so. Moreover, his tightlipped personal physician, Theodore Morell, was well-known in Germany for his effective treatment for syphilis.

There was also a powerful neo-pagan impulse in his hatred, adopted mostly from Richard Wagner, his favorite composer. He despised Christianity because of its Jewish roots, admired Buddhism, the occult, and, surprisingly, Islam. In the latter case, he was apparently unaware of the common foundation shared by Islam and Judaism. Lack of education may sometimes be embarrassing.

The violence against Jews took two forms: street hooliganism and pogroms in the first years of Nazism, and "legal" methodical violence of the state, which became dominant when Hitler came to power. Jews were forced to sell their property at a knock-down price to Aryan businesses. Nuremberg's decrees of 1935 stripped the Jews of their basic rights, and by 1938 their economic power was destroyed. The first concentration camp at Dachau was already waiting for its temporary tenants. When Herschel Grynszpan assassinated a German diplomat in Paris, Nazis organized a classic pogrom, murdering Jews, raping Jewish women, looting Jewish shops and burning down synagogues, which became known as the *Kristallnacht*. The similarity with the Russian pogroms was too obvious and embarrassing, so it was the last chaotic outbreak of anti-Jewish violence; from that point on it was the state which took over the responsibilities for the Final Solution under the general supervision of Heinrich Himmler. Jews were expelled from schools, their driving licenses revoked, and segregation laws enforced; sexual relations with an Aryan became a criminal offence punished by imprisonment in concentration camp. Jews were excluded from German labor regulations and in fact were worked to death. From 1941, the Jews were obliged to wear a Star of David; to avoid any ambiguity, the word *Jude* had to be added in its center. This made easier to enforce numerous restrictions and to explicitly separate the Jews from the rest of the population. The leader of the anti-Semitic propaganda was a weekly *Der Sturmer* run by Julius Streicher, with the main message being that the Jews, as a species, did not belong with mankind and had to be treated accordingly.

Still, there was the unresolved "scientific" problem: who was Jewish? The decree of 1933 implied that a person with a parent or grandparent of the Jewish religion was of non-Aryan descent. In 1935, a conference, attended by the government officials, the highest medical officers of the party, and the German Medical Association came to the conclusions that quarter-Jews were Germans but half-Jews were Jews, as "among half-Jews the Jewish genes are notoriously dominant". This was unacceptable for the Interior Ministry, which insisted on the earlier formulation and which was finally endorsed: the quarter-Jews were Jewish. In rare cases, reserved for soldiers in combat units or relatives of the Nazi elite, a special certificate could confirm that its bearer was of German blood. Hitler personally supervised this bureaucracy.

The following piece from a report of Minister of Justice to Hitler needs no comment: "A full Jewess, after the birth of her child, sold her mother's milk to a woman doctor and concealed the fact that she was a Jewess. With this milk, infants of German blood were fed in a clinic. The accused is charged with fraud. The purchasers of the milk have suffered damage, because the milk of a Jewess cannot be considered food for German children.... However, there has been no formal indictment in order to spare the parents, who do not know the facts, unnecessary worry. I will discuss the race-hygienic aspects of the case with the Reich Health Chief". The report was filed in 1942.

This elaborated system of control over the genetic purity could sometimes fail in an embarrassing way: several high-ranking officers managed to blur their Jewish ancestry, including Erich von Manstein, apparently, the most brilliant of the German generals of the war. Even the Germans could not maintain perfect bureaucracy and consistency. Except for a period of three years, from 1940 to 1943, half-Jews and quarter-Jews could be drafted into the German army. In 1939, one of them, Werner Goldberg, who was blond and blue-eyed, appeared in a Nazi recruitment ad as "the ideal German soldier". What a shame for the Aryan race. Field Marshal Erhard Milch, presumably half-Jewish, was the deputy of Hermann Goering, the Commander of the Air Force and number two in the Nazi hierarchy. In order to hide Milch's origins, Goering ordered to falsify his birth records and bluntly commented: "I decide who is a Jew and who is an Aryan."

How could such a cold calculating pragmatist as Hitler enter into a full-scale war first with England and France and then with Russia and the United States? The fatal decision to attack Russia, with its immense spaces, large population, and vast economic potential, made necessary the deadly war on the two fronts, and is therefore especially puzzling. Simple analysis of economic resources and manpower would show that, despite its highly professional military, Germany just could not win such a war. It seems that Hitler could not resist the temptation of exterminating European Jewry. Both Poland and Russia were home to millions of Jews; in Poland alone, nearly ten percent of the population was Jewish, which totaled to approximately three millions. Since the early thirties, Hitler had repeatedly claimed that, if a war broke out, the Jewish culprits would pay the price. He finally stated this explicitly at the beginning of 1939: "if international-finance Jewry inside and outside Europe should succeed once more in plunging the nations into yet another world war, the consequences will not be the Bolshevization of the earth and thereby the victory of Jewry, but the annihilation of the Jewish race in Europe". The pre-planned mass killing of Jews, his wet dream, was thus purposely displayed as resulting from their evil intrigues. Given the intensity of Hitler's hatred, it may be safely inferred that destroying European Jewry was among the central motivations of the war. He seemed to believe that the Final Solution of the Jewish problem would also resolve all the others; it later turned out that the Holocaust was the only goal of the war the Nazis had managed to realize.

The invasion of Poland on September 1, 1939, and the outbreak of World War II finally provided Hitler with the opportunity of mass systematic extermination of European Jewry. He wasted no time. Atrocities against the Polish Jews began immediately with the occupation but, in a few months, German pragmatism took over: Jews were concentrated in ghettos, mobilized and put to work as starving slaves seven days a week. Then, experiments were set forth to invent the most effective and convenient means of mass killing, a sort of killing industry. Hitler authorized the use of carbon monoxide in specially designed gas chambers of the death camps and was careful enough not to leave any written orders. With the invasion of Russia in 1941, Hitler was able to put his hands on the Jews who were still remaining in the territory overrun by the German army, almost a million and a half of them. Mobile killing units manned by the SS-troops, the so-called *Einsatzgruppen*, were assigned to the advancing army in order to exterminate Jews in an efficient way. In order to emphasize the importance of this mission, these battalions included lawyers and intellectuals, like Otto Ohlendorf, who had degrees from three universities. About the same time Hitler ordered mass extermination in the death camps specifically built for this purpose, mostly in Poland. The largest of the camps were: Auschwitz, Majdanek, Treblinka, Sobibor, Belzec and Chelmno. Altogether, there were almost two thousand concentration camps and nine hundred labor camps; a huge system of murder and slavery pedantically supported by the German governmental bureaucracy. Heinrich Himmler and Reinhardt Heydrich directed this machinery with Adolf Eichmann supervising its smallest details. The conference, which took place in a villa in Wannsee near Berlin under Heydrich's supervision, was to improve coordination and speed up extermination. The German railway system worked at full capacity transporting victims, tightly packed in freight-cars, from occupied territories in the East and in the West to their final destination, often at the expense of the military effort. Nearly six million Jews were killed; this was the only task Hitler managed to achieve "successfully" in the war he engineered. Mass elimination also included Slavs, Russians in particular, Gypsies, the mentally ill and homosexuals, though on a much smaller scale.

Religious Jews perceived what was happening to them as God's will; the very enormity and nature of the mass killings seemed to confirm this, as no human being could possibly be capable of committing atrocities on this scale and in this manner of ruthlessness. God once again was punishing Jews for their sins and for their breach of the Covenant, and there was no point in resistance. Jews were isolated, surrounded by a mostly hostile local population, had no weapons and could offer no significant resistance to the overwhelming force of the SS and the German army. The well-known uprising took place in the Warsaw ghetto in the spring of 1943, where Jews kept fighting for a month. Paul Johnson commented in his book that "some European countries, with well-equipped armies, had not resisted for so long". This however was a local event which could not slow down the death machinery.

Militant Zionists left Europe for Palestine prior to the war and then molded a core of the Jewish Brigade, formed with the help of Churchill in

1944; nearly thirty thousand Jewish volunteers from Palestine served in the British army. Altogether, a million and a half Jewish soldiers fought in the allied armies, nearly four hundred forty thousand of them in the Red Army. Operatives from the *Yishuv*, the Jewish settlement in Palestine, parachuted in occupied Europe; almost all of them were caught by the Gestapo and killed. The backbone of the worldwide Soviet spy network, (one of them was the famous *Red Chapel* which operated in Europe), was Jewish. One can only speculate what would have happened, if Germany would have fought for another year or two. Would the United States then have turned to the atomic option? As the atomic bomb was to a significant degree the creation of Jewish scientists, would this hypothetical and high-risk step have been interpreted as the Jewish revenge?

The atrocities were of such monstrous dimensions that the German people could not be unaware of what was going on; one million and three hundred thousand of them served in the SS alone. How was it possible for a Viennese vagabond, in a span of a few decades, to get control of the German destiny, fool this nation of great scientists, engineers, and composers, and plunge the world into the most devastating catastrophe ever? To put it simply, the Germans had been bribed; the myth of their racial superiority, which conveniently removed any moral restrictions, was one of these bribes. As Himmler put it: "One principle must be absolute for the SS man: we must be honest, decent, loyal, and comradely to members of our own blood and to no one else. What happens to the Russians, what happens to the Czechs, is a matter of utter indifference to me....Whether the other peoples live in comfort or perish of hunger interests me only in so far as we need them as slaves for our Kultur. Whether or not ten thousand Russian women collapse from exhaustion while digging a tank ditch interests me only in so far as the tank ditch is completed for Germany".

The victimized Jews were another bribe. The Germans profited enormously from the genocide: shopkeepers from eliminating a Jewish concurrent, industry from exploiting Jewish forced labor, banks from seizing Jewish capital, Nazi officials from looting Jewish property; concentration camps guards from being spared the Russian killing fields. Many Germans made their living by providing services to the enterprise, the railway system alone, busy in transporting the victims to death camps, employed a million and a half of them. The Holocaust was compensation, a prize, Hitler granted to his people for the murderous war over world domination which he masterminded.

With rare exceptions, German scientists and engineers provided the Nazi regime with their support, which allowed the industry to work at full capacity, producing advanced military hardware. With typical German discipline, "Aryan" medics and anthropologists participated in the national mania of racial superiority, measuring human skulls and experimenting with prisoners. Einstein's theory of relativity was tagged as a sample of Jewish physics. It may be safely stated that though Hitler was the main promoter of his cause, he was in turn guided and assisted by positive feedback on the part of the German scientific and cultural circles. There was opposition, but it was of minor scale and came unexpectedly from military brass and aristocracy.

Germany was not alone. Austrians skillfully avoided responsibility for their participation in the genocide; however, they were often the most enthusiastic instigators, organizers, and executioners. Cheering crowds and a national euphoria accompanied Hitler's annexation of Austria in 1938. Many high-ranking Nazis were Austrian, including Hitler, Eichmann, the man specifically in charge of extermination, and Ernst Kaltenbrunner, the last Gestapo chief. Commanders of four out of six central death camps responsible for the killings of three million Jews were Austrian. Still, after the war the Austrians had successfully managed to represent themselves as Hitler's victims.

Rumanians committed mass atrocities in Bessarabia, Transnistria, Odessa and Rumania proper. There were cases in which Rumanians would not take care of burying the victims even in the face of the fury of their pedantic German bosses. Ukrainians, Lithuanians, Estonians, and Latvians served in the SS killing units and were especially cruel as guards of the death camps. In France, there were ten active anti-Semitic organizations, including the Vichy government. They were ready to participate in the German campaign; nearly seventy five thousand Jews were deported from France and most of them perished. Italy did not have a tradition of deep-rooted anti-Semitism, the Italian fascism originally carried no special anti-Jewish luggage and Jews were among activists of the movement in its early stage in the twenties. Under the German pressure, racial laws were introduced in 1938, and Jews were interned in camps during the war. The situation worsened in 1943 with the German occupation of half of Italy. Most of the Italians refused to cooperate but nearly a thousand Jews were sent to Auschwitz anyway. Many thousands of Jews were killed in the Balkans and Belgium. Toward the end of the war, the unique Jewish community of Hungary, spectacularly successful in sciences and arts even by Jewish standards, lost half-a-million to the Nazis. The Dutch attempted to save their ancient Jewish community but more than one hundred thousand, nearly seventy percent, were deported and killed. A little known fact is that, in a paradoxical way, the Finns and the Bulgarians, Germany's allies, saved all of their Jews, two thousand and fifty thousand, respectively; the Danes ferried five thousand to Sweden at the last moment.

The Allies did little, if anything, to stop the death machinery, which operated at full capacity for about six murderous years. A recent study shows that as early as 1941, the British Intelligence Services knew about atrocities going on in Germany and occupied territories. Among the Western leaders, only Churchill tried to influence the events by ordering bombardments of death camps in the final stages of the war. It was too little too late. For Stalin, who harbored strong anti-Semitic sentiments, this was a minor issue deserving no special considerations. The Catholic and Lutheran churches, which had nurtured anti-Semitism for centuries, were mostly silent. Pope Pius XII knew perfectly well what was going on with the European Jewry and refused to intervene. After the war, the Vatican was busy helping war criminals to escape from Europe, in particular, to Argentina.

Though there were Poles, Germans, and other nationals, who literally risked their lives hiding Jews, in general, the population of the occupied territories cooperated with the Nazis or turned a blind eye. The French police handled deportation of French Jews to concentration camps; the same in the Balkans; French, Flemish, Swedes, Estonians and other European nationals volunteered for the Waffen-SS, the elite combat arm of the

SS-troops, and fought in the war alongside Germans. In 1938, the Polish government annulled Jewish passports, leaving Polish Jews in Germany trapped in the hands of the Gestapo. Jews who began returning to Poland after the war were greeted with the comments of "it is a pity that Hitler has not finished all of you off"; anti-Semitic riots erupted in Poland in August, 1945 and lasted for seven months; nearly four hundred Holocaust survivors were murdered. Even in Holland, a railway company cooperated with the Nazis in deporting Jews to death camps and then the local population benefited from abandoned Jewish property. There was also a phenomenon of *kapo*: Jewish collaborators, recruited by Germans to police the camps.

Jews had managed to recover after each major catastrophe. They even acquired new qualities: they came back from Babylonian exile and re-established their statehood; after the disastrous anti-Roman revolts, they preserved and enhanced their own spirituality; the expulsion from Spain led to the appearance of spiritual centers in Palestine, Arab countries and Eastern Europe. The flight of Jews from Russian pogroms assisted in the rise of the powerful American Jewry. Demographers estimate that without persecution and assimilation over a period of several millennia, there would be more than one hundred million Jews in the world today, a hardly imaginable situation. Nevertheless, the Jews did better than the others, as many nations have disappeared forever from the historic scene.

In the aftermath of World War II, Jews began to return to places associated with their most painful past, including Germany. In recent years, its government has done its best to attract immigration of Russian Jews. Presently the Jewish population there approaches two hundred thousand. But the focus of the Jewish response to the Holocaust was in Palestine. Jews had all the reasons in the world to finally grasp that their defense must be in their own hands; they needed a state of their own. Still the task ahead looked enormous, without any precedents and beyond the reach of humans. However, the scale of the catastrophe they had just undergone had also been without precedents and far beyond any imagination. For their sins they had been exposed to the fullest measure of God's fury, the time had come for God's blessing.

Return

Despite the French tradition of tolerance, anti-Semitism there was as deep and widely spread as in Germany. A chilling example was the Dreyfus' affair, which surfaced in 1895. Captain Alfred Dreyfus, the only Jewish officer serving on the French General Staff, was convicted of spying for Germany and publicly degraded in a humiliating ceremony in Paris under screams of the agitated crowd "Death to Dreyfus! Death to the Jews!". A little known Viennese journalist, Theodor Herzl, had witnessed the scene and, as a consequence, abolished his aspirations for Jewish assimilation. Within half a year, he had completed the draft of his book "*The Jewish State*", which would set forth the philosophy of political Zionism.

The very idea was not new. For thousands of years, a rebirth of Israel was at the very foundation of Judaism and passionately prayed for in synagogues. In the beginning of the seventeenth century, Rabbi Menasseh Ben Israel wrote in his letter to Oliver Cromwell: "the opinions of many Christians and mine do concur herein, that we both believe that the restoring time of our Nation into their native country is very near at hand". Mordecai Noah, an unknown American citizen, purchased Grand Island in Niagara River, New York, from Indians in order to found a Jewish refuge-state there naturally named Ararat; a spectacular corner-laying ceremony took place in the city of Buffalo in 1825. On this occasion, the orchestra performed *Judas Maccabeus*, an oratorio by Handel, and Noah declared himself the sheriff of the new-born state. Napoleon and Disraeli tried to promote a similar idea. All these attempts failed.

It was timing that made Herzl's book a far-reaching success. Emancipation in Europe, the emerging American Jewry, and a free capitalistic economy, which suited the hard-earned mobility of Jews and their talent for improvisation, enabled Herzl to revitalize the old idea. Herzl's basic assumption of wealthy Jews spending huge amounts of cash to finance the enterprise had quickly proven false. It took pragmatically-oriented minds of philosopher Max Nordau, scientist Chaim Weizmann and labor leader David Ben Gurion to attract impoverished and idealistic Jews from Russia and Eastern Europe as the hard core of the movement and thereby transform a somewhat naive idea into a political reality.

The word "Zionism" was coined by Nathan Birnbaum, an activist of Jewish student organizations in Vienna. The First Zionist Congress met at Basel in 1897. Herzl financed it from his own pocket and, to impress gentiles, took care to create a proper European style, such as black suits and white ties for the delegates from sixteen countries. As any event involving Jews, the gathering received wide media coverage with correspondents from twenty six newspapers present. German merchant Daniel Wolffsohn selected blue and white as the colors of the Zionist flag.

Herzl also toured Europe and undertook a series of meetings with European monarchs and government heads to promote his idea. To his surprise, the response was mostly positive though sometimes sarcastic: the Kaiser bluntly commented: "I am in favor of the kikes going to Palestine. The sooner they take off the better". The British were much friendlier and tried to help. They raised a possibility of settling in Uganda but it was rejected by the Zionist movement, especially by its militant Russian branch. Herzl summarized that: "Palestine is the only land where our people can come to rest". It was Orthodox Jewry which offered fierce opposition. For them, Zionism was a sinful intervention of secularized Jews, perhaps inspired by Satan, in God's scheme of Redemption. Rabbi Joseph Chaim Sonnenfeld wrote: "There is great dismay in the Holy Land that these evil men who deny the Unique One of the world and his Holy Torah have proclaimed with so much publicity that it is in their power to hasten redemption for the people of Israel". It took decades for religious Zionism to emerge and cooperate with the basically secular movement; sects of Orthodox Jews still adhere to their opposition.

Chaim Weizmann, a well-known chemist, invented a method for the production of solvent acetone needed for the British war machine and therefore enjoyed much influence in British political circles. Creation of a national Jewish home in Palestine was a subject of his talks with Lord Balfour during the First World War. The political atmosphere also favored such a move, as a large Jewish settlement in Palestine could provide useful services to the Crown, in particular watching over the Suez Canal. Besides the Arab opposition, objections came from influential Jews who saw the preferable option in assimilation. Eventually, in 1917 the declaration was formulated as a letter by Lord Balfour to Lord Rothschild, which stated: "His Majesty's Government views with favor the establishment in Palestine of a national home for the Jewish people, and will use their best endeavors to facilitate the achievement of this object, it being clearly understood that nothing shall be done which may prejudice the civil and religious rights of existing non-Jewish communities in Palestine, or the rights and political status enjoyed by Jews in any other country." The Jewish Agency was established in 1923 in order to encourage Jewish immigration to Palestine, land acquisition and strategy panning. The Jewish Agency was to play a major role in realization of Zionist goals in the Holy Land.

With the growing political chaos in Europe and rise of the Nazis, the influx of Jews to British-controlled Palestine, *Eretz Israel*, was steadily increasing as were tensions and clashes with the local Arab population. Charles Wingate, a brilliant British officer and devoted Christian, had trained Jewish "Special Night Squads" to confront Arab militants and thereby set forth the tactics of *Hagana*, the mainstream Jewish military organization. Hagana's fighters along with graduates of the British army, who had fought against the Germans during World War II, were to form the backbone of the Israeli army.

The British kept a tight immigration policy, pleasing the Arabs and drawing attacks from the armed Jewish underground. Six British paratroopers were killed in 1946, after which militants under the command of Menahem Begin blew up the King David Hotel in Jerusalem. The casualties included British, Arabs and Jews. Enough was enough. In 1947, the British announced that they were returning their Palestinian mandate back to the United Nations. Jews and Arabs continued attacking each other and the British. The latter retaliated by harsh measures, including the death penalty.

On November 29, 1947, the General Assembly endorsed a partition plan for Palestine. Jewish and Arab states were to be independent with Jerusalem as an international zone. This was a surprising move because powerful American and British oil companies traditionally opposed to the Jewish state. Persecuting Zionists in his own country, Stalin hoped that the Jewish state would become his power base in the strategically important Middle East. President Truman, who was moved by the Holocaust, adopted a Zionist position. It was a rare case of agreement between American and Soviet delegations, both of which supported the resolution. They even worked together on a schedule for British withdrawal. Nevertheless, when Secretary of State George Marshall heard that Ben-Gurion was to announce the independence of the State of Israel, he remarked that "the old man has lost his mind". On May 14, 1948, Ben-Gurion declared independence, which was immediately recognized *de facto* by Truman and then *de jure* by Stalin.

The Arabs rejected the partition, as stated by the resolution of the Arab League of December 17, 1947. They were bent on elimination of the *Yishuv*, the Jewish settlement in Palestine, once and for all, by military means. Azzam Pasha, Secretary General of the Arab League, bluntly announced on the radio that "this will be a war of extermination and a momentous massacre". Armed forces of five Arab countries led by the Egyptians, invaded Palestine, marking the beginning of the War of Independence.

After the War of Independence (1948–9) came the turn of the Six-Day War (1967) and then the Yom-Kippur War (1973), all of them initiated and lost by Arabs. Numerous clashes and military conflicts took place in-between, including the Sinai War (1956). For twenty two years, from 1978 to 2000, Israel fought the Lebanese War of varying intensity and in 1987–92 and 2001–4 fought against two successive Palestinian uprisings. These are impressive military records by any criteria. The wars were short but bloody, contrary to popular impression about the easy Israeli victories. In the War of Independence Israel lost 6,373 people, about one percent of its Jewish population at that time. In three weeks of the Yom-Kippur War, the losses per capita were roughly equal to American losses per capita during a decade of fighting in Vietnam.

The attitude of the United Nations towards Israel speaks for itself. When in 1947 the Arab League refused to obey the United Nation resolution regarding the partition of Palestine, this organization did not make a sound, but when the war resulted in the flight of Palestinians to neighboring countries, it swiftly established the Relief and Works Agency for Palestine Refugees, which had helped to perpetuate the problem. The United Nations did no such "favor" for many millions of European refugees in the wake of the Second World War or during the India-Pakistan War in 1947. A new peak was reached in 1975, when the General Assembly, led by such human rights champions as the Soviet Union, Arab and African countries, adopted a resolution which classified Zionism as a form of racism. It took sixteen years to abandon the resolution that became possible when the Soviet Union had finalized its own collapse. In a sense, the uniqueness of Israel as a state mimics the uniqueness of the Jews as a people.

Exhausted by the endless conflict, the two sides, the Israelis and Arabs, were looking for negotiations. After the bloody wars, humiliating defeats, and enormous losses, Egypt, the very heart of the Arab world, was the first to sign a peace treaty with Israel. More than half of the Jordanian population is Palestinian by origin that endangers the Jordanian Kingdom, which does not seek Palestinian domination. This makes the Kingdom dependent on Israeli support; Jordan was the second Arab country to sign a formal peace. A series of secret and semi-secret agreements between Israel and the Palestine Liberation Organization (PLO) culminated in the Oslo Accords, signed in 1993 with great pomp and optimism. The accords were loosely formulated; their authors generously mixed the harsh reality with wishful thinking and, in fact, gambled with the fate of the two peoples. A by-product of the euphoria which followed was the uncontrolled influx of thousands of Palestinians into Israel proper and in fact materialization of the Right of Return.

Two policemen, Na'il Suleiman and Yossi Tabeja, were teamed as a joint Palestinian-Israeli patrol to symbolize mutual cooperation in preventing terrorism. On September 29, 2000, Suleiman got out of his jeep, and at point-blank range, shot his Israeli partner dead. This was the beginning of the second Intifada. This full-blown but low-intensity war lasted for nearly four years. The Arab version claims that it was the visit of Ariel Sharon to the Temple Mount one day earlier, which triggered its beginning. Palestinians focused on suicidal killings of civilians in shopping malls, cafes, and buses, which clearly aimed to undermine the consumer-oriented, pluralistic Israeli society and thereby drive the Jews out. The conflict was, once again, about the very existence of the Jewish state in the region. The tactics of "targeted killings" of militants and their leaders was the Israeli response, which forced Palestinians to agree to a sort of ceasefire. The second Intifada claimed the lives of 1,330 Israelis and 3,333 Palestinians. Killing 515 Israelis, 144 suicide bombings were carried out. Not long ago, Ariel Sharon in a daring unilateral move initiated the evacuation of the settlements in the Gaza Strip. Another bold step was construction of the controversial fence separating Israel and the Palestinian Authority, whose consequences still remain to be seen.

Since the end of the forties, millions of immigrants have settled in Israel, including nearly seven hundred thousand Jews from Arab states who moved to Israel between 1948 and 1967, compared with approximately the same number of Arabs who fled Palestine. As a result, the ancient Jewish communities of Morocco, Egypt, Yemen, Iraq and Syria practically ceased to exist. A one million of Russian Jews settled in Israel after the collapse of the Soviet Union. Also, Israeli society changed from a predominantly Ashkenazi and socialistically-oriented to a liberal and pluralistic one.

Presently, Israel's population is estimated at about seven million, eight and a half times larger than it was at the time of the establishment of the state. Of these, 5,240,000 are Jews and 1,340,000 Arabs. At the time of the state's establishment only thirty five percent of the Jewish population was Israeli by birth; this figure is presently nearly sixty five percent. The economy became more open and market-oriented; this, however, backfired and led to widened economic and social gaps. According to a recent study, nearly one hundred seventy voluntary organizations are busy providing emergency food for half-a-million Israelis living below the poverty line. Israeli Arabs as well as Jewish Orthodox and new immigrants feel marginalized; many of them are impoverished and unemployed.

More than five million Jews live in the United States., but in a year or two most of the world Jewry will leave in Israel, the only country in the world to see significant growth in the size of its Jewish population. By 2020, there will be more than six million Jews in Israel. The number of

Jews is expected to decrease from three hundred eighty thousand to one hundred eighty thousand in the former Soviet Union. A million will live in Europe, twenty percent less than the present figure. The rate of assimilation should remain at the level of fifty percent in the United States and eighty percent in the former Soviet Union. In recent years, the number of Jews in the World has remained stable, at some thirteen million; no significant changes in this figure are expected in the near future.

Israel is a country of high-tech, advanced agriculture, and the sophisticated military; yet is also known for its long list of blunders; Israelis like to leave things as they are, hoping, often without any basis, that nothing bad will happen. Messianic factions of the religious minority may resort to violence and seem to pose a threat to Israel's existence. Israeli society is excessively pluralistic, if not fragmented, especially for such a small country; the gap between the rich and poor is on the rise; the high birth rate of the Arab population may change the demographic balance and thereby the very nature of the state. Indeed, in 2004, the average birth rate among Moslem women was 4.4 babies as contrasted with 2.6 for Jewish women. Given this statistics and the dangerous religious overtones of the conflict, no one-state solution advocated by Arabs and leftist activists appears possible.

The efficiency of the public sector is a problem, as the immigrants from Eastern European and Arab countries brought traditions of rigid governmental bureaucracy with them. According to a recent report of the World Bank, Israeli public services perform poorly if judged by Western standards: professionalism and credibility of governmental apparatus was rated 80.8 percent in contrast to the average of 89.7 percent for developed nations. The government corruption index is a scale which evaluates the public perception regarding the extent to which government power is not used for promoting private interests; Israel was again rated 80.8 percent as opposed to the average of 91.4 percent for the developed world. According to the same report, only 74.4 percent expressed confidence in the judicial system although the vote of confidence was 90.3 percent for Western countries. No surprise, it is slow and is often driven by the motivation to comfort "the system". It is not King Solomon's court. Given this situation and a national mania for endless disputes and arguments, it is only natural that Israel has the highest number of lawyers per capita in the world.

From a historical point of view, the modern Jewish state has so far been a success story, a transformation of the sleepy and forgotten Asian region into a modern state at the life span of one generation. The Israeli gross domestic product (GDP) per capita (nearly $25,000 in 2005) is about five times larger than that of Egypt and almost twice as large as that of the oil-rich Saudi Arabia. This is impressive but still well below the west-European average. A recent issue of *Red Herring*, business of technology magazine, published a list of the one hundred most promising European companies, twenty of which turned out to be Israeli, with Germany and France represented by ten names on the list. The life expectancy is among the highest in the world. Figures released by the UNESCO show that Jews still adhere to their love of the written word; thirty three million books were printed in Israel in 2005 for a population of roughly six million, which is among the highest rates in the world. According to a survey of 2004, seventy seven percent of Israelis define their health as good; eighty two percent of adults are satisfied with their lives. The last figure is amazing in view of permanent security concerns. At the same time, only forty seven percent of the adult population feels positive about the state of their finances.

The Other Side of the Coin

The Biblical stories of David and Goliath and Samson and Dalila, which dealt with the warfare between Israelites and Philistines, may be mistakenly interpreted as predecessors of the present Israeli-Arab conflict. The Philistines, who populated the southern coastal plain of what we call the Land of Israel and Gaza Strip for about six hundred years, were conquered by Nebuchadnezzer, exiled to Babylon and, unlike the Jews, vanished there. The Philistines were Indo-Europeans, consumed pork and did not practice circumcision, which is why they were referred to in ancient sources as "foreskins". They had only a single mark left in history: the name of the land "Palestine"; *Filastin* in Arabic was derived from the

Roman "Philistines" in the first century B.C. to eradicate any sign of the Hebrew presence. The Palestinians, who migrated to the region much later, are of different Semitic Arab origins. Regardless of genetic considerations, the plain fact is that their language, religions and culture, in other words, their memes are completely different from those of the Philistines.

Talking about similarity, it is possible to find a sort of it between Jews and Palestinians. The Israeli-Arab wars gave birth to Palestinian Diaspora. Also, as noted earlier, virtually everything concerning Jews becomes vague and controversial; the same can be said about Palestinians. The Philistines vanished without a trace but the term "Palestine" is very much alive, though it underwent really remarkable adjustments. For centuries it was a purely geographical term referring to the area roughly overlapping ancient Canaan, though a plan by the League of Nations treated most of modern Jordan as Palestine. The British Mandate of Palestine included what are presently Israel proper, the West Bank, and Gaza Strip. Curiously, Immanuel Kant, the German philosopher, referred to German Jews as "the Palestinians living among us". A person born or legally residing within the boundaries of the British Mandate, regardless of ethnicity or religion, was a Palestinian by British law. The English language newspaper, *Yishuv*, explicitly Zionist in orientation, was called *The Palestine Post* and only later renamed *The Jerusalem Post*. There never was a Palestinian state. The Palestine Authority, established in 1994, was supposed to control the Gaza Strip and most of the West Bank but so far has failed to do this.

Palestinians lived in the region for many generations, were deeply attached to the land and kept close family relations. In the course of the War of Independence, misguided by virulent and over-confident propaganda and also threatened by Jewish militants, many Palestinians fled to neighboring countries in the firm belief that a swift Arab victory and prompt return were about to come; they soon found out the true extent of the disaster. It was the *Nakhba*, the Palestinian Holocaust according to Arab interpretation of these events. However, it is difficult to ignore the fact that the Palestinians have turned down the offer of a state of their own, made in the end of the forties, and since then they have resorted to chaotic and irrational armed struggle as the only means of achieving their goals.

Pragmatic politicians point to the two critical issues preventing a reasonable solution to the present dangerous conflict: control over the holy sites in Jerusalem and the problem of Palestinian refugees. Though skillful diplomacy may resolve the first, the second indeed seems unbridgeable. The Jewish state treated the absorption of immigrants as a national goal. The Arabs, excluding perhaps Jordan, did everything possible to contain Palestinian refugees in temporary, badly maintained camps, and used them as a constant leverage against Israel.

As from the ethnic point of view, there is no appreciable disparity between Palestinians and Arabs from neighboring countries, this discrimination had obvious political reasons. There is no doubt that the issue was exploited by Pan-Arab streams to promote Arab unity and create a great Muslim state. There has been abundant evidence that Arabs are just incapable of dealing with the very thought of an Israeli presence in the region; the real motivation of the Palestinian policy has always been explicit or implicit refusal to recognize this state.

Palestinian camps in Gaza, Lebanon, Jordan and Syria indeed became sources of armed struggle against Israel. Their population dramatically increased due to the high birth rate of Muslim women, which further worsened conditions in the camps. There were unexpected results too, as these camps drew Israeli reprisals with destabilizing consequences for the host country. Arab rulers also failed to foresee that the camps were to become hothouses of international terrorism, a threat, mainly to Western-oriented Arab regimes. Presently, Palestinian militants are taking part in such far removed conflicts as Chechnya, Afghanistan, and Iraq. The Palestinian Authority is heavily handicapped by various militant gangs. The persistent Arab dodging of any reasonable resolution of the refugee issue has also been fertilizing the worst Israeli suspicions: Palestinians want to overtake Israel proper and do not want a state of their own next to it. Indeed, Faruk Kadumi, a prominent main-stream politician, admitted in a minute of frankness: "we do not want our state; we want the right of return". This disastrous evolution of the state of Palestinian refugees went on for decades under the umbrella of the aid program sponsored by the United Nations.

Could this happen in other places? As an example, consider the case of Sudeten Germans, a German-speaking ethnic group, which belonged to the multi-ethnic Austrian-Hungarian Empire. Gregor Mendel, the father of genetics, as well as the prominent Jewish personalities, Sigmund Freud, the father of psycho-analysis, Franz Kafka, the innovative writer, and Gustav Mahler, the famous composer, were, in a sense, Sudeten Germans. In 1918, in the wake of World War I, when the Empire was divided into several countries, the Sudeten Germans became a part of Czechoslovakia. Following the notorious Munich agreement, they were annexed by Germany in 1938. After World War II, more than three million were expelled from their homes, villages were destroyed, and nearly two hundred sixty thousand killed. No reverse influx (exchange of population, similar to the flight of Jewish immigrants from Arab countries to Israel) took place. Thus, the scale and circumstances of these events were much more severe than those in Palestine. However, Germany and Austria resettled those who survived and since then the issue has been stuck in endless negotiations and practically unknown outside of Central Europe. Another example: in 1945, millions moved between East Germany and Poland and all were resettled. Even more dramatic events took place in Asia in 1947: millions of Muslim refugees fled from India without any significant intervention by the United Nations. What has made a difference in the case of Palestinians and perpetuated the problem? It seems that anybody knows the answer: the Arab oil.

There is a controversy regarding a realistic estimate of the Palestinian population. According to the official figures released by the Palestinian Authority around three million six hundred thousand Palestinians, including one million four hundred thousand in the Gaza Strip, live in the territories; many experts view these figures as very inflated and suggest that some three million or even less would be more relaible.

As an intensely traumatic experience for Arabs, and the Palestinians in particular the very existence of the Jewish state seems to trigger modernization in the Arab world, which otherwise could still be submerged in apathy. Indeed, a United Nation report written by Arab experts, which was published in 2002, draws the following conclusions regarding the state of the Arab world: one in five Arabs lives on less than $2 per day, around fifty percent of older adolescents would like to emigrate, women (half of the population) are marginalized, the huge oil income of $3,000 billion over the past twenty years was mainly utilized to enrich the rich. According to a recent report of the World Economic Forum, population growth in the Arab world has gotten out of control and there is urgent need for radical governmental reforms.

However, given their great past and the magnitude of their human and natural resources, the Arabs have not yet spoken their final word and, in this sense, the full consequences of the creation of Israel are still to come into play for the Arab world.

2

Genes

The Jews: are They Human?

—Wyndham Lewis

Jews and Genetics

The Bible contained, among others things, details of Israelite genealogies, being in this sense a sort of the genetic document. The strict regulations of the marriage between close relatives and prohibition of incest seem to further stress the major role the Jews attached to heredity.

To this end, one may suggest that the Jews inherit their "otherness" from their parents as a trait, more or less in a way they may inherit brown eyes, speech defects, big nose, and faulty digestion. In order to ascertain this, it is first necessary to appreciate the basic laws of genetics, which is the subject of this chapter.

The Austrian monk, Gregor Mendel, was the first to take a decisive step in resolving the mystery surrounding inherited traits. Having studied mathematics at Vienna University, Mendel pioneered rigorous methods in plant breeding and in biology in general. He spent eight years, from 1856 to 1863, in the quiet Czech town of Brno, experimenting with common pea plants on a small plot of land of his monastery. He grew thousands of plants, keeping comprehensive records with German precision and dedication. In 1865, Mendel published his investigations, which explained experimental results by the existence of discrete factors appearing in pairs and passed on from one generation to the next; by doing that he founded the science of genetics, as we know it today. As usually happens, his theory aroused no substantial interest when published, though he took care to send reprints to prominent scientists. Mendel died in 1884 and could not know that he had opened a door to an entirely new and revolutionary scientific discipline of vital importance. In the early twentieth century, the full power of his discovery would become strikingly evident. His factors of heredity would be called genes and the structure of practically all human genes, their totaling number around twenty five thousand altogether, would be fully specified in the subsequent decades.

When genetics emerged as a major discipline, the Nazis tried to formulate their anti-Semitism as a respectable well-founded science and went on with experiments in the death camps. Since then, in view of the tragic results of the Nazi war against the Jews, no serious researcher could dare to approach the Jewish phenomenon from a genetic point of view.

In recent years, the situation has changed and there has been much interest in genetic facets of the Jewish phenomenon. The studies focused on the three issues. First, do the Jews posses genetic characteristics which may point to the existence of a common ancestor? In other words, does the Biblical version hold true? Second, Jews suffer, as other ethnic groups, from a set of genetic disorders. What is an explanation for this phenomenon? And, finally, what are the reasons for the extraordinarily high intelligence, on the average, of Ashkenazim? In general, is the Jewish "otherness" of a genetic or memetic origin? Considerations of this and the following chapters should help the reader to answer these questions by himself.

Genetic Software

Take, for example, such a trait as your hair color; it could be blond at your birth but you may loose this benefit and become brunet with age. Thus, what you actually have inherited from your parents is not a specific hair color but its pattern or plan to be fulfilled during your life span.

In other words, one inherits the information or recipe, which guides one's body and personality as they evolve from birth to death. It remains to figure out the way in which the recipe is stored in a human body and transferred from parents to offspring.

Mendel focused on such traits as seed color, which can be green or yellow, stem length, which can be tall or short, pod shape, which can be puffed or pinched, etc., and tracked their inheritance from parents to offspring. Each trait had only two alternative forms, which facilitated understanding the results. A natural reproductive process of the pea plants is self-fertilization, when the stamens (the male parts) drop pollen inside the same flower and fertilize the eggs of the pistil (the female part), which matures later on. This is called pure-bred reproduction unlike cross-breeding, which involves two plants. If you decide to study inheritance of traits, you should experiment with both versions.

Take two pure-bred plants with green seeds color and cross-breed them; this results in progeny of the same green color and is identical to pure-breeding. But what happens, if you cross-breed a green-seeded plant with a yellow-seeded plant? Will the offspring be of an "intermediate" seeds color? Mendel's experiments showed that no blending takes place. The seeds of the resulting plants will be all yellow. However, if you would go on for one more generation, the green seed would miraculously reappear.

It appears that the number "two" should play a significant role in analysis of heredity, just because there are usually two parents involved in a reproduction process. That is why Mendel's basic assumption about the existence of discrete heredity factors, *which appear in pairs*, the so-called genes, makes sense. Consider breeding between, say, two plants of the same green seeds, and assume that each of them has a pair of genes symbolically denoted as AA, which is in charge of this trait. Then the offspring can get a single gene, A, called *allele*, from each of the parents, and would again have the pair AA. This particular trait would be indistinguishable from both of its parents. The same holds true for yellow-seeded parents. If they have a pair of genes, BB, the next generation will collect the B allele from each of the parents, resulting in the same gene pair, BB.

A trait which is visible, like that, is referred to as a *phenotype*, while the underlying gene pair is a *genotype*. For example, the first experiment dealt with the green seed phenotype and the AA-genotype; the second experiment dealt with the yellow seed phenotype and the BB-genotype. A genotype, which consists of the same alleles, is called *homozygous*, so both of the above genotypes are homozygous. The genotype AA (BB) implies the green (yellow) phenotype.

Obviously, the next experiment should deal with a cross-breed between a parent with green seeds (AA genotype) and a parent with yellow-seeds (BB genotype), to get, as mentioned earlier, yellow-seeded offspring only. The "green" phenotype should disappear despite its presence in one of the parents. This can be explained by the same logic, namely, picking up the A allele from the parent of the "green" phenotype and the B allele from the parent of the "yellow" phenotype and concluding that the genotype of this generation is AB. As the latter consists of two different alleles, it is referred to as *heterozygous*. It follows that the same "yellow" phenotype may be due to either a homozygous BB genotype or to a heterozygous AB genotype; even though the genotypes are different, the phenotype is the same. Because the B allele appears in both, you may speculate that this allele is in charge of the yellow seed color, regardless of the genotype, and is therefore a *dominant* allele. The A allele, which manifests itself in the "green" phenotype only when it appears in the homozygous AA genotype, in other words, appears twice, is called a *recessive* gene or allele.

To examine the latter, grow a second generation by cross-breeding two parents of the previous one, in which both are of a heterozygous AB genotype. Suggesting once again that an offspring picks up alleles of the parents in a random fashion, you must conclude that, as far as its genotype is concerned, the following possibilities come into play: AA, BB, BA, and AB. Because AB and BA represent the same genotype, there are three different genotypes. Thus, the homozygous AA genotype, which corresponds to the "green" phenotype, indeed reappears. A simple count shows that for three cases of the "yellow" phenotype due to BB, BA, or AB genotypes, there should appear one case of the "green" phenotype, due to AA genotype. This is precisely what Mendel observed in his experiments. It became known as Mendel's 3:1 ratio.

In short, Mendel's breakthrough theory inferred: i) the inheritance of each trait is governed by genes, which are passed unchanged on to offspring; ii) for each trait, a plant randomly inherits one gene (allele) from each parent and thus genes come in pairs; iii) a particular phenotype may not show up in a plant but may reappear in the next generation; iv) independently assorted traits are governed by independent pairs of alleles. Further on, these basic principles of heredity will be shown to hold true for all complex life organisms, including humans.

At present, the point of view is that traits are influenced by groups of genes and not pairs alone.

Mendel's approach was ahead of his time and remained largely ignored until the early twentieth century, when other scientists came forward with a similar approach. Still, his hereditary factors seemed a pure abstraction without any real biological foundation. This impression changed when researchers improved their understanding of *cells*.

Genetic Hardware

Far back in 1665, Robert Hook, the same Hook who claimed that Newton stole the law of gravity from him, observed cork under a microscope and noticed pore-like structures, which he called cells. Theodor Schwann observed that living cells, regardless of their shapes, contained a stained body, a *nucleus*, which, in turn, as subsequent studies showed, included fiber-like curved creatures presently known as *chromosomes*. Figure 1 shows a cell enclosed by its membrane, together with the nucleus and chromosomes, the surrounding *cytoplasm*, and the so-called *mitochondria*, an organelle responsible for producing energy.

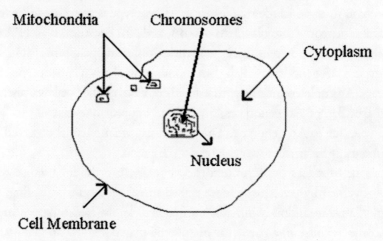

Figure 1. Structure of Cell.

The membrane and cytoplasm protect the cell content and allow for cell cooperation; chromosomes in the nucleus are carriers of genes; mitochondria are in charge of energy processes.

The fact that the number of chromosomes in a cell varied from one species to another but kept constant within the same species implied that chromosomes were inherited and thereby could carry genes. This was clearly a bridge between Mendel's theory and Hook's discovery made almost two hundred years earlier. The cell, nucleus, and chromosomes had emerged as basic carriers of life.

The human sex cells, sperm and egg, which are called *gametes*, have a set of twenty three chromosomes; such a cell is referred to as a *haploid*. Body or *somatic* cells have twenty three pairs of chromosomes; such a cell is referred to as a *diploid*. We have forty six chromosomes: each of our parents grants us a set of twenty three chromosomes, containing in their gametes.

As we grow from the fetus state to adulthood and then die, trying in between, amidst other difficulties, to reproduce, a cell with its chromosomes undergoes fairly dramatic changes. In particular, a body cell replicates itself by dividing; it first gives rise to two daughter cells; the latter produce four cells, and so forth. Observations have shown that during this process, known as *mitosis*, chromosomes behave like pre-programmed robots. They first duplicate themselves and then perform a complicated dance inside the nucleus' membrane, pulling it apart. Finally, the cell splits into two daughter cells, each having the same twenty three pairs of chromosomes. This is how we evolve, starting from a single fertilized egg, to a human, a many-trillion-celled structure: "omnis cellula e cellula", which in Latin means "all cells arise from other cells". (It may be noted that not all cells reproduce, including cells of central nervous system; which is why it is highly recommended to take good care of them.)

Now I can go over to a structure of the chromosome. Its simplified model is a linear sequence of loci, something like a string of beads. Each locus is associated with a certain function; for example, in the case of a plant, there is a locus in charge of flower color. Therefore, from a functional viewpoint, the locus represents a gene earlier introduced in a notional way by Mendel.

Since in the case of sexual reproduction, two parents contribute their genes, it is logical to arrange the chromosomes in pairs, coupling similar chromosomes. Figure 2 shows such a pair, the so-called *homologous* chromosomes, one chromosome from one parent, carrying, among others, a locus of gene responsible for flower color. Another typical feature of a chromosome is a presence of a condensed region, a sort of knot, near the middle of chromosome, known as *centromere*.

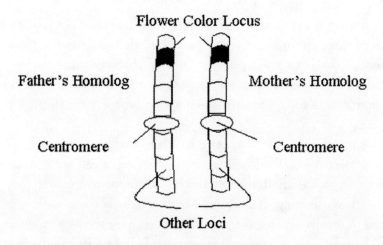

Figure 2. Homologous Pair of Chromosomes with Color Locus.
Genes are aligned along chromosome like beads, each having its own responsibility.

The previously mentioned mitosis holds true for our body cells. Gametes, which are sex sells, have a different structure and behavior. These are players in the drama of fertilization of the egg by the sperms and their fusion. If each of the gametes had twenty three chromosome pairs, their union should end up with forty six chromosome pairs. Then, if the process of mitosis held, these chromosomes would duplicate and be followed by division of the sex cell into two daughter cells, each having forty six pairs of chromosomes. This does not happen, which points to a fatal flaw in these speculations, as Theodor Boveri indeed figured out in a series of experiments with worms in the late nineteenth century. He showed that mitosis does not apply to sex cells. The sex cell is a haploid; it has a total of only twenty three chromosomes, half of those in the body cell. In the reproductive process called *meiosis*, which consists of pre-programmed duplication and a concerted "dance" of the chromosomes inside the nucleus, the sex cell undergoes two divisions and divides into four sex cells, each containing one set of the chromosomes. It is during this process that similar chromosomes of male and female parties intertwine and randomly exchange genetic material for the upcoming offspring to inherit. We can only envy this magnificent consistency of the mechanism of heredity.

The chain of these events is shown in Figure 3: first, sperm penetrates egg, producing a fertilized egg, called a *zygote*, a diploid containing two haploids of sperm and egg, respectively; then mitosis spurs the organism to reach its adulthood as a female or male. These may, in turn, produce a haploid of either egg or sperm, respectively, and so on.

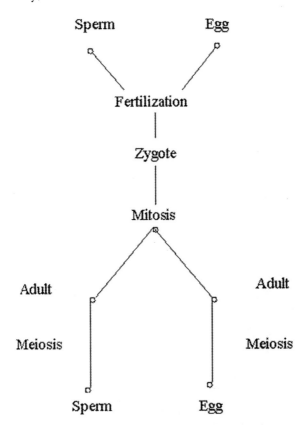

Figure 3. Chain of Alternations.
Male sperm and female egg produce a fertilized egg, called zygote. This then develops in either female or male adult, depending on randomly inherited special sex chromosomes.

There is no magic in the number twenty three. Our body cells have twenty three gene pairs just because this is what geneticists observe through their microscopes and no other explanation for this particular number is presently available. For example, body cells of worms have twenty chromosomes (their sex cells have ten). Until 1955, it was "well-known" that humans had twenty four pairs and that is why. In 1921, a Texan named Theophilus Painter was lucky to get his hands on the testicles of two black men and one white man, all of whom had been castrated for being found insane. After slicing proper sections and examining them visually through a microscope, he counted twenty four chromosomes in their spermatocytes. Because a sex cell is a haploid, body cells should have twice more, twenty four pairs. There was a case when scientists terminated their research with human liver because they could count only twenty three pairs of chromosomes in a cell, contrary to the observation of Painter. It took almost thirty years until Albert Levan and Joe-Hin Tjio, making use of refined techniques, showed that there are, in fact, only twenty three pairs. This time it was final.

Mendel dealt with the heredity of traits in pea plants such as seed color. But what can we say about gender, which is perhaps the most intriguing and precious of our possessions? Do parents influence the sex of their progeny as they influence, say, skin color? Is sex inherited as a trait, implying that a proper mechanism is also hidden in the chromosomes? Investigations of fruit flies provided the answer to this question.

Fruit Flies, Chromosomes, and Gender

In the beginning of the previous century, Nettie Stevens, a brilliant American geneticist, looked at the chromosomes of meal worms and noticed a strange short chromosome appearing solely in mail worms. It was denoted as a Y chromosome. Later its counter-part, the X chromosome was identified in both, male and female worms. This led to a critical discovery: the male gene is associated with a pair of XY chromosomes, the female gene with a pair of XX chromosomes. Males produce sperm with either an X or Y chromosome and females produce eggs with X chromosomes only. This clearly implied that the gender is a trait, controlled by the male, who donates either an X chromosome for a female or a Y chromosome for a male. Since then, it has become customary to refer to the X or Y chromosome as a sex chromosome and to the rest of them as *autosomes*. Though human body cells contain twenty three pairs of chromosomes altogether, only a single pair handles the gender.

Sex cells have a different structure than body sells. Females have twenty two autosomes and the X chromosome in their egg cells; males have twenty two autosomes and either the X or Y chromosome in their sperm cells. When fertilization takes place, the egg and sperm cells unite; the first cell of a baby will have a total of twenty three pairs of chromosomes. The set of chromosomes of a human male with twenty two pairs of autosomes and a pair of sex chromosomes is shown in Figure 4. A female has the same set with the Y chromosome replaced by the second X chromosome.

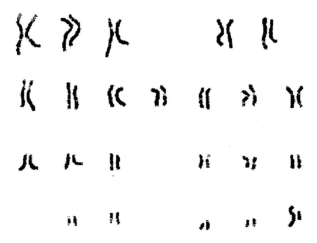

Figure 4. Set of 46 Chromosomes of Body Cell of Human Male with Sex X and Y Chromosomes Paired in Right Lower Corner.
Courtesy: National Human Genome Research Institute.
Each homologous pair is matched by length, centromere location, and functional responsibility. Female gets second X chromosome instead of Y chromosome of male; cells of egg or sperm have only 23 chromosomes.

A set of twenty three chromosomes still could not be responsible for enormous variety of inherited human traits. Though chromosomes were bearers of heredity, they could not be taken as the elementary units corresponding to the abstract Mendel's units of heredity. It became clear that they should contain smaller and more numerous structures. Genes were yet to be found.

History of genetics is full of exciting stories of discovery, which often seem like a thriller with genes being a main personage pursued after. Dramatic events surrounding a research team headed by Thomas Morgan belong in this category. This group conducted extensive investigations of inheritance in a common fruit fly named *Drosophila melanogaster* and was therefore known as the Fly Lab. *Drosophila* was chosen for its high fecundity; it also has a short life cycle, and large numbers could be taken care of at no great expenses. Indeed, financial support of basic science was a rarity at those times and Morgan and his students housed the insects in small milk bottles that they had stolen from apartment steps.

Identification of the meaningful traits of *Drosophila* was far more difficult than finding the obvious phenotypes of garden pea plants; Morgan would regularly warn his colleagues that "the flies will always fool you". For about seventeen years, in a smelly and dusty room, Morgan and his team scrutinized thousands of flies. Morgan would often draft his data on the back of old envelopes beautified with fly remains, even though a special etherized morgue had been set up.

The breakthrough came when Morgan's group caught a male fly with white eyes. This was a *mutant*, which contrasted with the standard red-eye flies. Cross-mating between this white-eyed male and a normal red-eyed female produced red-eyed progeny only, but the white phenotype reemerged in the second generation in the 1:3 ratio, precisely as predicted by Mendel. It was not the end of the story though, as, surprisingly, these white-eyed flies were all *males*; white eye females were found only in the third generation. In the light of the previous work of Stevens, this meant that an allele responsible for the white eye is physically located on the X chromosome; indeed, if this allele were on the Y chromosome, then no females could get the white eye. The allele was recessive, as this color reappeared in the second generation; the white-eyed females apparently had two copies of the recessive allele. This was the triumph of Mendel's theory and a historic moment in the understanding of heredity.

Morgan's Fly Lab made other key discoveries, among them the effect of linked genes, which are genes inherited together as a gene package. Making use of the concept of linked genes and their "crossing over" from one homologous chromosome to the other, they managed to construct the first genetic map for *Drosophila*, the fly which became a star of genetics. Over ten thousand flies were examined for this research.

According to the Torah, God made Eve from Adam's rib, which should have equipped her with both, the X and Y chromosomes, unless, during the fabrication, God had cared to "improve" the design by putting the Y chromosome aside and "installing" the X chromosome instead, which he did. Eve was lucky, because the Y chromosome bears genes mainly associated with maleness, for example, those responsible for sperm production or hair in nostrils. The Y chromosome is also short. There are speculative theories claiming that this chromosome is doomed to vanish in the evolutionary process; only females will survive and develop a system of asexual procreation. Even though this may not be so, to the delight of the feminists, the genetic structure of the female seems to suggest more versatility and sophistication than that of the male.

Jewish Odysseus and Two Mutations

Darwin's theory of evolution and natural selection seemed to contradict Mendelian genetics: if inherited genes are in complete control, there is no place for change. It was the concept of mutation which provided a bridge between the two theories. The above mutant white-eyed fly could be a result of a random "bug" in a gene. Indeed, living organisms spend their limited time on earth under varying, often violent conditions, which can cause random genetic changes. The latter are then inherited by the progeny, of which only the fittest survive.

One of Morgan's students in the Fly Lab was an eccentric biologist, Hermann Muller; this very short, bald New-Yorker, son of a Jewish mother, felt his ideas were not properly referred to in the Fly Lab publications and privately hinted at anti-Semitic sentiments on the part of his boss, as a reason. It is not clear at all whether this was true. Whatever the case, Muller quit his work at the Fly Lab and, for a while, moved from one university to another in the best of Jewish tradition. Amid this wandering, he had formulated a theory of spontaneous mutation and conducted experiments dealing with the genetic effects of X-rays. These were to be later proven as a landmark in genetic research but brought him little recognition at the time.

Muller also harbored leftist beliefs, fashionable among intellectuals in the period between the two World Wars. He embarked on what may be called Odysseus' journey of our time. Europe in those years was already under a heavy cloud of the upcoming Second World War, with the Communist regime in Russia and the growing Nazi movement in Germany. Millions were trying, often by risking their lives, to flee the shaking old continent for the United States. But Muller, saturated with ideas of social justice and equality for all, left the United States for Europe, swimming precisely against the stream. He spent a year in Germany and managed to leave just about when Hitler came to power there. Muller moved to the Soviet Union but his stay there turned out to be a perfect case of being in the wrong place at the wrong time: Trofim Lysenko, the official, politically correct Russian biologist, initiated an anti-genetics drive, which soon became a central subject of the campaign of the Communist Party. Soon, some of Muller's co-workers began to disappear mysteriously. Indeed, there was no point in scientific arguments if you could get your opponents shot. Rumor had it that Muller went as far as writing letters to Stalin to no avail. Eventually, he left Russia for Europe and, needless to say, took part in the Spanish Civil War as a member of the leftist International Brigade. He eventually returned to the United States but there was little interest in hiring an obscure scientist with such a history on his back and a possible FBI file. In 1945, a disillusioned Muller accepted a professorship at Indiana University, only to receive the Nobel Prize within a year for his earlier investigations of mutations induced by X-rays.

Artificial mutations pioneered by Muller were to play a crucial role in witty experiments staged by geneticists in years to come. Natural mutations take place spontaneously, because our cells are subject to all the fury of our habitat, which may cause random alterations in so delicate a creature as a gene. Our progeny inherit these modifications and, in turn, may produce variations of their own. At some point, natural selection comes heavily into play and only the fittest survive. Therefore, mutations, as understood by Muller and other scientists, may be a component in the evolution of the species, providing a bridge between the two apparently contradicting theories, Darwinian selection and Mendelian genetics. According to Darwin, nature produces more organisms than can survive and only those with favored characteristics endure and may pass them on to their offspring. Mendelian genetics seemed to exclude variations from one generation to the next, but they may be explained by mutations.

Another contributing factor to the evolution is a prolonged biological association between different species, known as *symbiosis*; this theory was promoted by Russian botanists Konstantin Merezhkovsky and Andrey Famintsyn at the end of the nineteenth century and later by Iwan Wallin, an American anatomist. Wallin was especially interested in symbiosis involving bacteria; in 1927, he wrote: "It is rather startling proposal that bacteria, the organisms which are popularly associated with disease, may represent the fundamental causative factor in the origins of species". In any case, the role of mutations in the occasional appearance of new strains of viruses is indisputable; for example, American scientists have recently established that the flu virus, which killed millions worldwide in 1918–9, shares common mutations with the bird flu presently spreading over the world; the latter may therefore be potentially devastating.

Everybody is born with a few mutant genes out of about the twenty five thousand available. In the majority of cases, a few faulty genes cause no harm because body cells have in fact twenty four thousand gene pairs. If one gene malfunctions, then the other copy can take over. This may bring about unexpected phenomena. An example is a condition known as *thalassaemia*. In its severe form, it is due to a pair of faulty genes in charge of hemoglobin production, which results in heavy anemia; a minor version, resulting in mild anemia, is caused by a single deficient gene. Paradoxically, carriers of this gene provide a poor habitat for the malaria parasite and are therefore immune to malaria. So, in malaria-infested regions of Africa, individuals with the deficient hemoglobin gene have better chance of survival. They pass it on to the next generation so that populations of such regions have a higher frequency of anemia cases.

Human mutations, when combined with proper social circumstances, may boost major historical upheavals. I will illustrate this with an example of how an inherited mutation in a British family backfired in Russia and probably changed the course of history. In fact, it appears that *two* independent mutations were simultaneously involved in the affair.

Followers of a Christian sect of British Israelites believe that the British have their roots in one of the Lost Tribes of Israel and speculate about a possible bloodline between King David and the British monarchs, which, softly speaking seems highly controversial. What is known for certain is that there was a bloodline between the British and Russian royal families: Russian Tsarina Alexandra, the spouse of the last Russian Tsar, Nicolas the Second, was a granddaughter of the English Queen Victoria. After giving birth to four daughters, the Tsarist couple was especially happy when at last an heir, their son Alexis, was born. Regrettably, he had hemophilia, a bleeding disease. The latter could be tracked to the British royalty. Although the daughters and granddaughters of Queen Victoria showed no signs of this illness, her male offspring had hemophilia. This was the link to the Tsarist family. Mendelian analysis of this case shows a sort of similarity with the white eye trait in the fruit fly investigated by Morgan's group. Female family members, including the Queen and Tsarina, were only carriers of a mutated sex-linked recessive allele responsible for blood clotting and located on a sex X-chromosome. However they passed this trait on to males who did develop hemophilia.

Alexis' potentially fatal illness was to have far-reaching consequences. Desperate and intensely religious Tsarina turned to Grigory Rasputin, a mystic healer, to cure the ill heir and provide spiritual services for the Tsarist family. According to rumors, Rasputin had had troubles with the law since his youth in Siberia. Once, he narrowly escaped from the ruthless hands of local peasants, who accused him of horse stealing. Those peasants could not have cared less about legal issues and were about to lynch him when a policeman suddenly arrived at the scene. Rasputin ran away and, after wandering around and staying at remote monasteries, traveled abroad, visiting, among other places, the Holy Land. He eventually showed up in St-Petersburg in 1911, where he successfully promoted himself as a Holy Elder (*staretz* in Russian) possessing extraordinary healing and spiritual powers. Bearded and firmly built, he was rumored to have exceptional sexual qualities and noble women were said to have had intimate relations with him. It does not seem plausible that Tsarina was among them, but her relations with Rasputin were very close. Tsarina claimed that he only could stop Alexis' bleeding and prevent the fall of the Russian empire. The destiny of Alexis, the family, and the whole of Russia were in the hands of this man of God. In a few years, Rasputin would hire or fire ministers and other governmental officers and, as many claimed, direct Russian policy. The inescapable Jewish "ingredient" was also present: making use of Rasputin's connections, his secretary, Aaron Simanovich, tried to improve the attitude of Nicolas II towards the Russian Jews.

Rasputin's rise infuriated the Russian aristocracy, which saw him as a primitive dirty peasant abusing their women and exploiting the weakness of the Tsarist family amidst the disastrous consequences of the ongoing World War I and social unrest. He was clearly putting the nation and the monarchy in danger.

When plotters, led by Prince Feliks Yusupov, lured him over to the Prince's palace, trying to assassinate him, they soon discovered it was not going to be easy. Knowing Rasputin's gastronomical preferences, they fed him heavily poisoned wine and tea cakes in absolutely lethal quantities, which should have killed him on the spot, but he merely felt groggy and murmured something about the strange taste of the wine, so Yusupov shot him through the chest. Still, Rasputin, even after being poisoned and shot, tried to get away. The determined conspirators had to shoot him again several times, beat him up, and eventually throw him into a hole in the ice of the frozen Neva River. Medical examinations of his corpse indicated that he had still been alive for some time under the ice. It appears that, besides Alexis' hemophilia, there had been another mutation involved in these dramatic events: Rasputin himself, whose personality remains a mystery up to this day.

Nicolas II, a fairly helpless Tsar, could still hold his throne, if provided with the firm support of the Russian nobility, governmental apparatus, and the military. This was not to be the case however, as the vital components of the monarchy were in complete disarray as a result of the corrupt influence of Rasputin's affair. Nicolas II was left alone amidst the catastrophic Russian war effort and his fall was inescapable. Eventually, Bolsheviks took over and the Tsarist family was deported to a remote Siberian city and brutally murdered. Aftershocks of these events were to be felt by the entire world in the decades to come.

This story seems unique in illustrating radical effects of genetic mutations on human history. Another possible example of such an effect is the extraordinary and horrific personality of Hitler, as discussed earlier. In 1918, he, as a soldier, was badly affected by a gas attack and temporally blinded. This could well have genetic consequences and gave rise to speculations which represented him as a mutation.

A by-product of genetic studies was the naïve idea of breeding humans with improved traits and at the same time discouraging reproduction of genetically-disable individuals, especially those with mental illnesses. This approach became known as *Eugenics*, which postulated that humans should be dealt with like livestock, without any considerations of spiritual, social and environmental factors. The Nazis adopted this idea and, with their Teutonic dedication and ruthlessness, tried to find its place in their theory of pure race. The horrible nature of the Nazi regime and, especially, experiments, which took place in concentration camps and involved Jewish prisoners, delivered a fatal blow to Eugenics as a legal scientific approach. It may still return to the spotlight with advancement of human cloning.

Sex and Helix's Cryptogram

Chromosomes could be observed via a simple optic microscope, which says nothing about their chemical structure and functioning. As to genes, at this stage they remained a vague object speculatively defined by their Mendelian attributes. Unexpectedly, observations of urine color were proved instrumental in making further progress. In general, urine color is often indicative of the state of our health, from the common cold to fatal infections. Dark urine may be a sign of the *inherited mutation of alkaptonuria*, an innate metabolic defect. Archibald Garrod suggested back in 1902 that a faulty biochemical process controlling liquid wastes was responsible for this disorder, thereby implying the possibility of genetic chemistry. In other words, if genes are in charge of heredity and, if what we inherit is information, then genes should contain information; if an inherited trait, like alkaptonuria, were indeed due to chemical effects, a gene involved should contain information in chemical form. It took four decades for experiments to prove Garrod's idea.

Geneticists often deal with what can be called very elementary living organisms, such as pus, fungus, bacteria, flies, viruses, etc. Although being not particularly attractive to work with, such organisms have an important advantage: they reproduce much faster than Mendel's pea plants. *E. coli* bacterium, for example, reproduces in four hours and a fruit fly in two weeks. Yet, the results are usually applicable to humans. It was common bread mold which helped to elaborate and sharpen Garrod's suggestion. This mold is a haploid (its cell has only one copy of each gene, no need to differentiate between a recessive and dominant allele) and needs only the so-called *minimal agar* to support its growth. The agar contains salts, sugars, and the vitamin biotin. Under normal conditions, the mold produces enzymes (proteins) transforming the above chemical substances of the minimal agar into amino acids and other compounds needed for its growth. This underlies the chemical nature of metabolism.

To begin with, George Beadle and Edward Tatum, two American biologists, using Muller's idea, "knocked out" some genes of the mold by X-ray radiation and then observed the termination of its growth. This implied that the damaged genes stopped providing information necessary for the enzymes' production, because the minimal agar was still there. The subsequent major key finding was that the mutant mold did resume its growth provided that the proper enzyme was added to the agar as a supplement in order to compensate for a missing substance.

Beadle and Tatum were able to sort out the effects of each of the enzymes, and established the crucial rule that "*one gene supplies information for making one protein*". They thereby formulated the fundamental, chemical definition of a gene as a code for the production of a single protein. Since, in this case, the trait was a vital metabolic function, not just a phenotype, this was a major improvement of Mendel's definition of a gene as an abstract hereditary factor.

Still, the chemical structure of genes remained a puzzle. Back in 1869, Friedrich Miescher experimented with pus collected from infected bandages and managed to separate a chemical substance extremely rich in nuclei, the so-called *nuclein*, a concentrated soup of nuclei and, thereby, chromosomes. Chemically, nuclein was a mixture of nucleic acids and proteins. Thus, it was assumed that genes, which reside on chromosomes, should be made either of the former or the latter. Due to the greater variety of possible forms and, subsequently, greater capacity for carrying information, protein chains were first thought to be chemical substance of genes, but investigations pointed to the deoxyribonucleic acid, DNA. The story of this discovery is as thrilling as a good Hollywood movie.

We may get pneumonia from a bacterium called *Pneumococcus*. There are two strains of this bacterium. One strain, say, the V-strain, is virulent and another, say, the H-strain, harmless. Like the fruit fly, *Drosophila*, or bread mold, this bacterium was destined to bring about a breakthrough in genetics.

In 1928, Fred Griffith had indeed observed that the V-strain killed mice in a few days, but the H-strain was neutralized by the immune system and left mice healthy. Then, Griffith heated a culture with the lethal V-strain so as to kill the bacteria; when injected into mice, this *heat-killed* V-strain did not cause any infection. He then injected both the heat-killed V- and the standard H-strains to other mice and was surprised to find that this mixture of two presumably innocent strains was lethal. He had found the *live* bacteria of V-strain in the blood of the dead mice, which certainly were not supposed to have been there. Griffith naturally assumed that *something* had been transferred from the heat-killed V-strain to the H-strain, causing metamorphosis of the latter. He noted that the transformation was stable and was passed down from one generation to the next. In other words, it behaved as a Mendelian trait.

Griffith left the nature of the above "something" a challenging mystery. In the forties, Oswald Avery, Colin Macleod and Maclyn McCarty broke the heat-killed V-strain into its elementary chemical units: sugar coat, protein, DNA, and RNA and by a systematic elimination of neutral substances had made a landmark discovery: the "something" was the DNA of the V-strain. In other words, the DNA had survived the heat shock and, when the H-strain bacteria were around, it rendered them lethal. This became known as the transforming ability of DNA and clearly implied that DNA was the carrier of genes; in fact, *genes are merely made of the DNA.*

During meiosis (the replication process of sex cells) similar chromosomes, one of a father and one of a mother, intertwine and exchange genetic material. This is what sex is about, if we set aside the emotional and ceremonial facets of this activity. It turns out that bacteria also have "sex". As was discovered by Joshua Lederberg in the forties, bacteria couple and then transfer their DNA through a mating channel to produce a next generation. Lederberg had followed the approach of Beadle and Tatum, using *E. coli* bacteria instead of bread mold. When subject to radiation, the bacteria could not produce enzymes to trigger production of the four substances necessary for their survival: methionine, proline, threonine, and biotin. Imagine that you have mutant bacteria A, which cannot produce methionine and biotin, and mutant bacteria B, which cannot produce proline and threonine. So, both mutants are doomed. However, if you mix them together and wait for awhile, you surprisingly get a colony of bacteria, which thrives from generation to generation. Thus, one mutant has supplied its genes to the other, allowing each of them to complete the set of needed substances. The mechanics of gene transfer was found later: the mating bacteria, which belong to two different groups, or, in a sense, genders, develop a pilus, (the term for a channel between them), which allows for a flow of genes from one mate to the other.

Viruses, it turns out, have "sex" with bacteria in the following manner. Alfred Hershey was investigating viruses, the so-called *phage*, which attack bacteria if the latter are around. His group had shown that a virus would sting bacterium with its tail and then use it to pump genes in the form of DNA into the host. The genes instruct enzymes of the host to trigger reproduction of new viruses. The bacterium thereby becomes merely a phage-maker. It is a manifestation of the same transforming ability of the DNA, which was first investigated by Avery's lab for the *Pneumococcus*.

A similar encounter may occur between a wasp and a spider. A female spider wasp can prepare a nest chamber for her larvae and then move to seek a spider in trees or on the ground. The spider may be several times larger, but the wasp with amazing skill stings it and injects poison, which contains genetic material, namely DNA. Then, the wasp drags the spider, the paralyzed victim, to the burrow, lays eggs on its stomach and seals the chamber with the spider inside serving as a breeding culture for her off-spring. As these illustrations of the transforming ability of the DNA show, this acid is the key to heredity.

The structure of DNA still remained unknown until, in the middle of the twentieth century, the emerged X-ray crystallography paved a way for one of the most crucial turning points in science ever, marked as the *double helix*. It had been known for some time from experiments of Phoebus Levene that DNA building blocks, the so-called, nucleotides, consisted of sugars, phosphates, and one of four nitrogen bases: adenine, A, thymine, T, guanine, G, and cytosine, C. In 1953, James Watson and Francis Crick, making use of X-ray data of Rosalind Franklin and Maurice Wilkins, published a classic paper detailing the structure of DNA. They found that its molecules are built in a form of a twisted ladder (double helix), with sugars and phosphates aligned along the uprights and coupled bases serving as the rungs. The genetic information is in the rungs, each of which contains either couple composed of A and T or a couple composed of G and C in an alternating order.

There was more to the story of the DNA structure. The spectacular discoveries and subsequent celebrations were not without the admixture of bitter rivalry, intrigues, and personal tragedy typical of humans. The brilliant chemist, Franklin, had come from a distinguished Jewish family; her great-uncle Herbert Samuel had been the first High Commissioner for the

British mandate of Palestine. It was Franklin who originally pointed out a helical structure of the DNA molecule and estimated its dimensions; regrettably, she did not rush to publish her results. She had tense relations with her colleague Wilkins, who tried to treat her as an assistant though she was a peer. He went much further and, without Franklin's knowledge, showed the results of her crucial experiments to Watson and Crick, the competitors from another University, which allowed the latter to finally put their model together and publish the stunning paper. It appears that there was a sort of plot based on personal ambitions and gender discrimination. In those times, a female scientist could easily fall prey to her biased co-workers. Franklin's role was underplayed by other actors of this drama, though with time, her crucial contribution became increasingly obvious. She died of cancer at age thirty seven and could not be there when Watson, Crick and Wilkins received the Nobel Prize in 1962.

At this stage, the structural chain of heredity looked like this: a cell contains the nucleus, which contains chromosomes, which in turn host genes made of DNA; the latter is built like a twisted ladder. Chemically, DNA consists of sugars and phosphates and the four nitrogen bases, A, T, G, and C. Each rung of the ladder is composed of two bricks, either a pair A and T or a pair G and C, so that the ratio of A/T and G/C are the same; the ladder's uprights made of sugars and phosphates keep the assembly together. Since a cell replicates either by mitosis or meiosis and contains DNA in its nucleus, the latter must replicate too. Watson and Crick suggested that one strand of the DNA molecule served as a template for recreating the other strand. This would conserve the same ratio of A/T and G/C and would mean that the new DNA is a copy of the old one.

Only one step was needed to eventually find out about the chemical structure of a gene. Human beings are mainly proteins, which underlie practically all of our biological functioning; for example, hormones, neurotransmitters, and enzymes are proteins. The proteins are made of twenty different amino acids, which our body must produce to allow for normal life. How does our body know which amino acids to produce? The answer was found in the structure of the DNA; that is where the mysterious power of the DNA stems from. Its bases, A, T, G and C are responsible for issuing proper instructions. In other words, there should be particular combinations of the bases corresponding to particular proteins. Since there are twenty amino acids and only four bases, a simple one-to one correspondence between a base and a protein would not work. Sometimes, elementary calculations may bring about fairly fundamental results and the following is an example. Assume the existence of an elementary informational unit, the so-called *codon*, consisting of an ordered sequence of three out of the four bases. Then there are $4^3=64$ possible triplets, which is more than sufficient to encode twenty amino acids (note that a sequence of two bases will not do as $4^2=16$). In the sixties, Marshall Nirenberg, Har Khorana and Robert Holley showed in an experimental way that this was indeed the case; for example, the GTA-triplet is an instruction of producing valine, whereas the ATG-triplet directs a body to produce methionine. They also figured out the role of another acid, the mRNA, as a "postman" which delivers messages from the DNA to amino acids.

Thus, *a codon encodes a particular amino acid.* Because a protein consists of ordered chains of amino acids, this is a sequence of codons, which encodes a protein. Recalling at this point that Beadle and Tatum found that one gene is in charge of one protein, it becomes clear that the gene is a sequence of codons. In the fifties, Fred Sanger, a British geneticist, and other scientists developed experimental techniques for a systematic discrete sequencing of amino acids in protein chains and, in turn, sequencing of associated codons, in other words, genes. It turned out that a gene sequence has its beginning and its end, a start-codon and an end-codon, just like a piece of good communication engineering. Thus, the gene is indeed a discrete message written with the help of four DNA bases grouped in codon's triplets. The DNA strands also contain empty regions between the genes, which carry no information about protein production; the functions of these empty intervals are still unclear. Similar regions exist also within genes.

The human genome consists of around thirty thousand genes; most of them have already been identified by scientists. The fact that each cell contains the same DNA does not mean that all the cells are identical; there are sex cells, egg or sperm, nerve cells, muscle cells, etc., which obviously function in dissimilar ways. If cells are to perform differently, it is because different genes are active in different cells. For this purpose as well as for the processes of their decay and growth, cells maintain the "off-on" machinery. Decay and death of cells at a proper rate are as vital as their division and growth, as the case of cancer illustrates.

To get further insight into the enormous complexity of the heredity organization, note that, besides its own double helix, DNA is also coiled in a larger scale around scaffolds, the so-called, *histones*. A tiniest chromosome of only two micrometers may package a DNA-coil of fourteen millimeters. A British geneticist with enhanced culinary interests sarcastically commented that an average meal provides nearly ninety thousand miles of DNA.

Though a strand of bacterium's DNA is almost filled with genes, the greatest part of human DNA, more than ninety five percent, does not contain genetic information. The full consequences of this are not clear at this point. Yet, this is not the end of the story of genes. Co-workers in Morgan's Fly Lab thought of genes as beads fixed on a string-like chromosome, which was obviously a simplistic visualization. Indeed, in the forties, the American biologist, Barbara McClintock, discovered that fragments of DNA can literally jump from one position on a chromosome to another. The truth is that we just do not know as yet what the end of this thriller may possibly be.

More of Genetics

As a preparation for the subsequent considerations of "Jewish" genetics, it is worthwhile summarizing relevant aspects of heredity and broadening our appreciation of it. This time, I will go in the opposite direction, from DNA to chromosomes and then to cells. Only one-and-a-half percent of the human DNA encodes manufacturing of proteins. There are at least twenty-five thousand genes or the encoded pieces of DNA. The elementary unit of encoding is codon, which is a triplet of the bases: A, T, G, and C.

The phenotype is a visible trait, or in its generalized interpretation, it is a gene effect (expression) on health, appearance, or a biochemical process. The genotype is a combination of alleles associated with a particular phenotype. A recessive allele expresses itself if it is present on both chromosomes. A dominant allele needs to be present only on one chromosome to affect the phenotype. Thus, there is a difference between the presence of a gene and its expression.

The experiments, I previously mentioned, were by necessity conducted under controlled conditions, which do not always fit the real world. The present viewpoint is that genes interact with each other. Genes' interaction depends on the environment; consequently, both, genes and environment come into play in shaping our health and personalities.

Genes lie on chromosomes. In body cells, there are forty six chromosomes, of which twenty three came from your father's sperm and twenty three from your mother's egg. In particular, female body cells have forty four autosomes and two copies of the X-chromosome; male body cells have the same number of autosomes, one X-chromosome and one Y-chromosome. Egg cells have twenty two autosomes and one X-chromosome; sperm cells have the same number of autosomes and either an X- or a Y-chromosome. At conception, sperm penetrates the egg and they form the first cell of a fetus, which again has forty six chromosomes and which is equipped with all the genetic material needed to develop in a human.

If chromosomes are stained with dyes or fluorescent substances, you may observe different patterns associated with proper sequences of the DNA. A single set of twenty three chromosomes contains our genome; each of us is a package of two genomes, which employ six billion base pairs of DNA. In turn, chromosomes are a part of a cell. Our body consists of trillions of cells. Even though all cells, excluding red blood cells, have the same genome, they are equipped with machinery to turn proper genes on and off.

Genetic mutations are merely an illustration of the optimistic Murphy's Law: "Anything that can go wrong will go wrong". In other words, faulty encoding can prevent production of a proper protein and thereby affect the health as well as appearance of an individual. Besides mutations, there are variants of DNA sequences, which do not significantly affect an individual and are present in at least one percent of the population. These are called *polymorphisms*. The human genome contains many millions of the so-called *single nucleotide polymorphisms*, or SNP. The SNPs may result from genetic diseases or may represent pieces of junk DNA, which does not carry explicit functional responsibility; as such, they are used for population studies, in particular, the migration of ethnic groups. In this context, they are usually referred to as *genetic markers*. DNA of the Y-chromosome bears persistent markers along paternal lines and the mitochondrial DNA along maternal ones. Among others things, genetic markers have been used to study migration of Jews.

Genetics specifies what we call a family in a definitive way: one half of the genes of a family member are shared with the mother, the other half with the father. Similarly, we share one-quarter of our genes with each grandparent. Zooming out of the family, we arrive at the population, which is defined as a collective of individuals, which may engage in interbreeding. This leads to formation of a larger set of alleles, referred to as the genetic pool. One genetic pool may differ from another in the frequency of certain alleles.

Genes of different species show striking similarity: there is a significant overlap between genomes of humans and that of the fruit fly. As deplorable as it is, we share almost ninety eight percent of the DNA sequences with chimpanzees, the genetic code of which was deciphered in 2005. A team of researchers identified around three billion building blocks of this DNA. One of the scientists remarked: "We now have the instruction book of our closest relative...". Yet, it is difficult to precisely pinpoint areas responsible for the differences between the two species, which appear to have split about six million years ago; for example, areas in charge of speech and upright walking. Altogether there are some forty million such differences and this is still ten times greater than the differences between two humans. Thus the work ahead is extraordinarily vast. Scientists assume that genes, which control mutual organizations of cells, make the difference.

One of the studies compared the genomes of fifty-two highly variable populations from Eurasia, Africa, East Asia, Oceania, and the Americas and found that 99.9 percent of the examined DNA was sequentially identical. This is why evolutionary biologists persistently point to the existence of a common ancestor for all living organisms, perhaps even inorganic one. This is represented as an absolute truth proving that there was no divine intervention in the creation of the universe.

The notion of perfect cognition contradicts to Judaism, as well as two other main religions, which admit uncertainty or even a mystery. What is absolute is the lack of absolute knowledge. It is sufficient to recall that only fifty years ago the well-known fact was that humans had twenty four pairs of chromosomes. The above version of the evolution theory assumes that the degree of divergence between the species can be measured by a simplistic account of disparity of their genomes. However, even a small disparity between the genomes, may lead to an enormous qualitative difference between the species. American thinker William James wrote that: "There is very little difference between one person and another, but, what little there is, is very important".

Jewish DNA

DNA is subject to evolution, for example, by mutations and polymorphisms, as was noted earlier and, thus, it bears its own history. This became particularly clear from studies of special chromosomes situated in cytoplasm, outside the nucleus, in energy producing organelles known as mitochondria. In the twenties, an extravagant American anatomist Iwan Wallin, mentioned earlier, noticed that the size and shape of these chromosomes resemble those of bacteria. Now scientists argue that billions of years back, the mitochondrial chromosomes were indeed free independent bacterial organisms. Later they were accommodated by higher cells for the mutual benefit of both parties.

As DNA is inherited, it stores everything which is biologically relevant, like the computer's hard disc. Even though you would take care of systematically erasing data, messages, and files, somehow they remain on the hard disk in one form or another, so that a professional, given time and resources, could find out what was going on with your computer. The same is true of DNA. An expert can, at least in theory, recover a history of the DNA-carriers from parents to their offspring. A Spanish team recently initiated an investigation into the national origins of Christopher Columbus. Incidentally, one of the speculative theories claims that he was a Jewish convert. The researchers are focusing on the Y-chromosome, which is thought to bear genes of maleness, inherited by a son from his father.

Jewish people, with their long entangled history and distinctiveness, seem to present a particularly interesting case from a genetic viewpoint. The first question to arise is their genetic identity. Are the Jews today genetically similar to their Biblical ancestors despite the gap in time and space? Do they represent a genetically cohesive collective, pointing to common ancestors? Alternatively, are they clustered by cultural and religious attributes only?

It was earlier noted that weak mutations, usually referred to as genetic markers, could be used for tracing ancestry. American geneticist Michael Hammer and his group investigated eighteen DNA markers, relying on comparison of the Y-chromosomes of nearly one thousand four hundred Jewish and non-Jewish males from Europe, Asia, and Africa. For the Jews, the scientists found a significant overlap, even though they came from various countries, like Morocco, Italy, Russia, Poland, and Iraq. This pointed to the existence of a common ancestor. According to the Bible, the ancestor should be Abraham; but Abraham also fathered the Arabs. Markers had indeed showed genetic similarity between Jews and Arabs. The genetic disparity between, say, the European gentile population and the Jews was found to be much larger than that between Jews and Arabs. So, as stated by the late Pope John Paul II, Jews are perhaps older brothers of Europeans, but mainly from a spiritual point of view; their closer genetic brothers seem to be the Arabs. As usual, Jews are one of a kind.

Another outcome of the studies was indication of a possible high adherence of Jewish women to Jewish men, at least for reproductive purposes: there was only about half-a-percent of admixture per generation with

Europeans. Sex with non-Jewish partners, however erotic and passionate it was, left a minor genetic trail per generation.

Anybody who accepts the Covenant and Old Testament can become a Jew. So, how can we explain this genetic uniformity? It seems that there was a shortage of volunteers to convert to Judaism, which can be easily understood. In periods of wars and revolutions, Jews were often the first to die, which further narrowed down their genetic variations.

There was, however, an exception. Around 600 C.E., the Turkish tribe of Khazars established its mighty state in the steppe between the Black Sea and the Caspian. Among others, they systematically harassed neighboring Slavic kin groups; the Khazars even appear in verses of the national Russian poet, Alexander Pushkin. Due to political circumstances, the royal family and aristocracy adopted Judaism and governed the state by Jewish laws for about five hundred years. The physician, Karl Skorecki, and his team found evidence that a certain Y-chromosome pattern was present in both, a small subgroup of Ashkenazi Jews and people from the Volga River of the Russian steppe. Overall, the studies conducted so far seem to point to genetic coherence of the Jews as a people, attesting to the veracity of the Bible in this regard.

Another relevant issue, raised and studied by Skorecki at the end of nineties, had to do with the tradition of Jewish priesthood. Around three thousand years ago, as the Bible has it, God summoned Moses to the top of Mount Sinai to receive instructions in the laws of the Covenant. Among other things, Moses was told that his brother, Aaron, and Aaron's sons, Nadab, Abihu, Eleazar, and Ithamar, would be set apart from the people and would be God's priests, Cohanim in Hebrew. From that time, these duties would be inherited by the male offspring: "And it shall be for them an appointment as Cohanim, forever, through all generations". God went on and described the ordination's ceremonies into the priesthood and other formalities in detail. So, Aaron was the first High Priest. If Jews fulfilled these instructions, then the DNA of the male descendants of Aaron from that time up to these days should have characteristics in common. Cohen is also a Jewish surname, in fact the most common one, which facilitates identification of the genetic lineage; by estimates, there are presently around three hundred fifty thousand Cohanim. Moreover, as only males can be Cohanim, studies may focus on the Y-crhromosome, which a son inherits from his farther. What makes it particularly interesting is that Cohanim may belong to various Jewish communities spread over the world and may look completely different; still, according to this tradition, they are supposed to have common genetic patterns. Obviously, if such characteristics do exist, this would indicate adherence of the Jewish people to the Biblical directive and not the divinity of the Bible

Initial data showed that a particular pattern of the Y-chromosome was indeed present in many Jewish laymen and mainly absent in Cohanim; but this finding had limited implications. It also provided no indications as to when the separation of the genetic patterns of laymen and priests had occurred, though, according to the Bible, it took place about three thousand years ago. A recent, more detailed study, which made use of twelve Y-chromosome markers, delivered a more definitive message: a pattern, the so-called *Cohen modal haplotype* (CMH), was frequently observed in the DNA samples of Cohanim and frequently absent in Jewish laymen. Significantly, the Ashkenazi Cohanim and Sephardic Cohanim, had the CMH in a proportion of around ninety percent, if only stable markers were accounted for.

Also, the markers used belonged with two groups: one group consisted of sequences, which change slowly, perhaps, once in human history since Adam. The other group contained less stable sequences, which can change in a generation. These two groups, one serving as the "hour hand", the other as the "minute hand", may be considered as a molecular clock. This clock showed that the separation took place several thousand years ago, with fairly good correlation to the Bible.

It must be noted that the genetic research provided evidence only concerning the common origin of Jewish people, not a perfect proof. Recent studies also show that the CMH is not unique for the described Jewish group and can also be found in significant proportions in Kurdish population of Northern Iraq, among others. Does this mean that Kurds are even in closer genetic kinship with Jews than Arabs?

A tribe of the Lemba populates a region adjacent to South Africa and Zimbabwe; tribesmen look like typical black Africans and speak Bantu. Nevertheless, for generations they have nurtured a tradition of being descendents of a lost tribe of Israel and observe Jewish customs, like circumcision, dietary rules, and the Sabbath. They claim that a prophet named Buba delivered them out of a devastated Israel after the revolt of Bar-Kochba. On their way, the Lemba first arrived in the city of Senna in what is present-day Yemen and then went on to Africa. English historian, Tudor Parfitt, took this story seriously and embarked on a sort of Indiana Jones journey to check its validity. He claimed to have located ruins of Senna in a remote corner of Yemen. The next step was to collect DNA samples from the Lemba people. When analyzed, the data showed that ten percent of them had the Cohanim's set of genetic markers; significantly, no other tribe around had this set. The data, when restricted to descendants of the prophet Buba, showed that an incredible fifty three percent carried these markers. The coincidence of the two factors, traditions and DNA, makes strong evidence for this case. It seems to be an amazing story of a tiny tribe which, over a few millennia, presumably lost their original phenotype but which appears to have preserved both, the spiritual beliefs and DNA.

Recently, another group, which also sees itself as a lost Israeli tribe, was reported by the media. The Israeli Chief Rabbi ordered the mass conversion to Judaism of a few thousand Indian people named Bnei Menashe, which means Children of Manasseh. To a certain degree, their traditions mirror the Jewish ones. The American Mormons and Ethiopian Falasha also declared their Hebrew ancestry, though genetic studies support no such claim, pointing to the West European origin in the former case and African in the latter one.

Jewish Genetic Diseases

Everybody has a few mutant genes, which usually does not cause any problems. These genes are "silent". Still, there are cases in which such genes fail to produce functional proteins relevant for a normal health. When inherited, lack of such proteins can lead to major damage to one's health, the phenomenon known as a genetic disease.

There are genetic disorders which occur among Ashkenazim almost ten times more frequently than in general population; Sephardim, also have genetic diseases, though to a lesser degree. A traditional explanation for this phenomenon was that the forceful concentration in ghettos and practice of intermarriage within small city communities, *shtetles*, prevented the influx of "foreign" genes. Another theory pointed to the so-called population bottlenecks that resulted from the atrocities against the European Jews. Still, a recent study suggests that the traditional occupation of European Jews in areas requiring elevated intelligence, such as money transfer, brokerage, management, and crafts, rather than, say, agriculture, was triggering a genetic mechanism, which encouraged the survival of faulty genes.

Autosomal dominant inheritance takes place when a single copy of a mutated gene is physically located on one of the twenty two autosomal chromosomes and manifests itself (expresses) in a genetic disease. As a child gets only one copy of a gene from each of the parents, the chance of inheriting the disease from a single affected parent is fifty percent; if both parents are ill, this chance is one hundred percent. Such disorders affect both men and women to the same degree and are passed from one generation to the next. There are cases when parents are healthy but alteration takes place for the first time in the egg or sperm participating in the conception of a child.

A different situation prevails in the case of *autosomal recessive inheritance*. Both of the copies of a mutated gene must be present for the disease to express itself. Parents, each having only one copy, are carriers, not patients; they are healthy and normal. There is a twenty five percent chance for the child to be affected by getting both copies of a mutant gene, a twenty five percent chance of inheriting two normal copies and fifty percent to receive one normal copy.

Turning to the sex chromosomes, note that a gene located on the Y-chromosome may be inherited by males only, unlike a gene located on the X-chromosome, which may be inherited by both males and females. It has therefore a relatively limited capability of replication. The Y-chromosome is also short and bears genes which are mainly typical of maleness. That is why this chromosome is sometimes referred to as a genetic wasteland.

The remaining case is an abnormal gene physically located on the X-chromosome, which may lead to the so-called *X-linked recessive inheritance*. The arising possibilities depend on the gender of the carrier. I will start with a male and then consider his offspring in order to cover all the possibilities.

As I noted earlier, a male cannot pass on a faulty gene located on his X-chromosome to his sons, as they get only a Y-chromosome from him; his sons therefore get nothing harmful for the following generation. The male, however, may pass on a damaged gene to all his daughters, as they receive one X-chromosome from each of the parents. These daughters may again pass on the gene, this time to both, grandsons and granddaughters, in equal proportion. Only the granddaughters will bear the damaged gene without being affected, because they have a back-up copy of it on their other X-chromosome which was donated by a healthy father. The grandsons, however, do not have such a defense, as their other sex chromosome is the Y-chromosome; they can be affected by the disorder.

The additional genetic mechanism responsible for genetic disorders is called the *skewed X-inactivation*: a female may have only one mutated allele but still be affected by the illness. In order to understand this phenomenon, note that males and females normally produce the same amount of protein; because a female has two X-chromosomes as opposed to one X-chromosome in the male, she develops a protective mechanism which blocks the expression of one of X-chromosomes in every cell of her body. When this mechanism malfunctions, the female develops a disorder.

Essentially, the picture is as follows: males are usually affected by an X-linked disease, while females are carriers only; male to male transmission does not take place, but affected males are in danger of passing it on to their grandsons via daughters who are carriers. An example is hemophilia discussed in the above in the context of the Tsarist family; other similar cases are color-blindness and the so-called G6PD deficiency due to skewed X-inactivation.

Most of the Ashkenazi genetic illnesses are of the autosomal recessive type and lack efficient cure. Symptoms of Gaucher disease, which is most frequent, include a deficient nervous system, bone degeneration, enlarged spleen and liver; its carrier frequency is around 1/10. If treated properly the patients may have a normal life span. Tay-Sachs may be lethal by the age of four; the patient suffers from paralysis, blindness, and brain degeneration; its carrier frequency is 1/26. The so-called familial dysautonomia manifests itself in blotched skin, excessive sweating, and cold hands and feet, developmental delays in speech and motor skills; its frequency is 1/30. Breast cancer has the frequency of 3/100. Canavan disease is mostly lethal by the age of four; the patient suffers from brain degeneration, seizures, and physical retardation; its carrier frequency is 1/40. Mental and physical retardation and death by age three result from Niemann-Pick disorder, type A; the carrier frequency is 1/70. Finally, small size at birth, poor immunity, increased cancer risk and sun sensitivity are symptoms of Bloom disorder; it is usually lethal by age of twenty seven; its carrier frequency is 1/100.

A blood test that screens for all of the Ashkenazi inherited diseases simultaneously is known as Ashkenazi Jewish Genetic Panel (AJGP); it enables one to find out, if there is increased risk of giving birth to a child with a genetic disease. The test is available for anyone upon request.

Sephardim have genetic problems of their own which are mostly those typical of host populations. Beta-thalassemia is caused by an insufficient amount of hemoglobin, as mentioned earlier; its carrier frequency is 1/30. Symptoms of Familial Mediterranean Fever include attacks of fever, lung inflammation, and arthritis, which can be followed by kidney failure; its carrier frequency may be as high as 1/5. Another disorder is Glycogen Storage Disease, Type III, the name which speaks for itself; it leads to liver problems and muscle weakness. It affects North African Jews with a carrier frequency of 1/35. All of the above illnesses are autosomal recessive. An X-linked recessive disorder is the above Glucose-6-Phosphate Dehydrogenase Deficiency (G6PD), which causes a hemolytic anemia.

Ultra-Orthodox Jewish communities in Israel and abroad were at particularly high risk, because of the habitual intermarriage assisted by a matchmaker; prior genetic screening of the candidates which is available today seems to reverse the situation. If results are not favorable, the match-maker can prevent the marriage.

It appears that prior genetic tests bring about significant improvement. In recent years, cases of the fatal Tay-Sachs disorder in the United States and Israel have been rare. Ten babies were born in North America with this disease in 2003, not a single one was Jewish; one such baby was born in Israel.

Marriages among various Jewish ethnic subgroups, first of all between Sephardim and Ashkenazim, which are widely common in Israel also broaden the Jewish genetic spectrum. The Israeli population shows a variety of phenotypes, as can be easily observed by a visitor walking the streets of Tel-Aviv or Jerusalem, and is comparable in this regard with diverse populations in large urban centers of the United States or Europe. A high rate of Jewish-gentile intermarriage in the United States, which recently reached nearly fifty percent, has the same effect. However, the progeny of such couples generally consider themselves non-Jewish.

The Costly Ashkenazi IQ

As follows from the above, the hard fact is that Ashkenazim suffer from genetic disorders which may be uncommon in host populations. Another hard fact is that Ashkenazim, on the average, perform very well in the *Intelligence Quotient* (IQ) tests. How it is that one ethnic group seems to be more intelligent or smarter than the others? The very question contradicts the generally adopted view that all people are genetically equivalent and even it seems racist and provocative. Nevertheless, ignoring the reliable statistical data available would not help, nor would avoiding the fact that certain genetic disorders are unusually frequent among Ashkenazim.

The IQ, designed so as to characterize a person's cognitive ability relative to a certain group, can also be treated as a trait. Popular techniques normalize the average IQ in an age group as one hundred and use the so-called bell curve to describe the IQ-distribution. The common opinion is that the IQ-scores evaluate school performance and academic achievements; there is also firm evidence that they correlate with other characteristics such as health, income, and job performance. Though a variety of tests are available for different cognitive abilities, all of them are underlined by what is known as the *g-factor*, which estimates general intelligence. Unexpectedly, social and nutritional causes, except for extreme cases of malnutrition, were found to affect the g-factor only slightly. This supported the view that the g-factor is heritable trait. especially if measured for adults. Moreover, recent studies tend to interpret the IQ as a biological variable, which may be subject to genetic manipulations. This being the case, scientists argue, the IQ should also be linked with natural selection.

Ashkenazim score to fifteen points above the mean value of one hundred in the IQ-tests. It is worthy of note that the difference of the averages implies a much greater disparity between higher IQ-scores. Calculations show that Ashkenazim, given the average of one hundred ten points and the standard deviation of fifteen, account for twenty three individuals per thousand having an IQ greater than one hundred forty, while gentiles only three. There is other convincing evidence to point to what may seem as politically incorrect but which is correct factually: the Ashkenazi contribution to the world science and culture is dramatically asymmetrical to their population. Constituting about three percent of the United States-population, Ashkenazim have won twenty seven percent of the Nobel Prizes in science. The Turing Award presented annually by the Association for Computing Machinery (ACM) is widely recognized as the Nobel Prize of computing; Ashkenazim have won twenty five percent of these awards. Ivy League is an association of top private American universities, known for academic excellence and elitism. Americans of Italian ancestry account for about nine percent of the population and only three percent of the Ivy League students; Jews account for twenty three percent. They also account for half of the World chess champions.

East and South Asians also perform above average in science and technology, though not as strongly as Ashkenazim. A similar phenomenon seems to exist in India, where the Parsi people, an endogamous group, have a history of long distance trading, management, business, and academic achievements and also a high frequency of Parkinson disease.

The controversial recent study by Gregory Cochran, an American population geneticist, and his team sets forth a theory claiming that the high Ashkenazi intelligence is a result of natural selection and that their sensitivity to genetic illnesses is a by-product. A traditional explanation for the set of Ashkenazi inherited illnesses was population bottlenecks in their past resulting from anti-Jewish atrocities. The authors of this research, with the help of statistical analysis, dismiss this theory as invalid. They claim that patterns of the Y-chromosome, mitochondrial DNA, and shared rare mutations, indeed point to the Middle Eastern roots of Ashkenazim. However, after the eighty or so generations, a significant proportion of the Ashkenazi genome had become close to European, despite the minor influx of "foreign" genes per generation noted by Michael Hammer and Karl Skorecki. This would not be the case if population bottlenecks had had any sizeable effect. Cochran's group also disapproves of the theory that Ashkenazi disorders are somehow connected with religious studies.

Cochran's team suggests that competition in trade, crafts, product-promotion, money lending and exchange, the traditional fields Jews were forced to pursue, was intellectually much tougher than routine agriculture. Consequently, a smart person had a better chance of making money under hostile conditions and raised more children, thereby passing on intelligence genes. Anti-Jewish regulations ensured that these genes would not escape to the genetic pool of a host.

Their theory goes further, claiming that biochemical mechanisms at the genetic level, which are in charge of high intelligence, are close to those responsible for inherited illnesses, like Gaucher or Tay-Sachs. Thus, by this theory, the enhanced intelligence has paradoxically nurtured faulty genes.

It is well-known from physiological studies that the unique capabilities of human neural system owe much to cells' connectivity. Engineering theory of networks also implies that higher connectivity means better performance. There is, however, a limit: too much connectivity and uncontrolled growth of cells may be harmful. Cancer is the best illustration of this effect. Theories of artificial neural networks also show that if connectivity exceeds a certain threshold, it becomes a problem. The inherited diseases, Tay-Sachs, Gaucher, and Niemann-Pick, all involve overdeveloped connectivity of nerve cells; on the other hand, patients do show high intelligence. In case of Gaucher's disorder, the only one which is not lethal, there is evidence that patients have a substantially higher IQ then the average. Of two hundred fifty five Gaucher patients, treated at Shaare Zedek Center in Jerusalem, nearly fifteen percent were engineers or scientists, while for the general Ashkenazi population it is slightly above two percent. Scientists predict that a heterozygote, in other words, an individual who inherited only one copy of a damaged gene should show enhanced intelligence, but a homozygote, who inherited both copies (from both parents) will also develop the illness.

It is possible to summarize Cochran's arguments as follows: i) as Jews were subject to persecutions during a difficult eight hundred years in Northern Europe, laws of natural selection favored the most intelligent and successful individuals to work in areas demanding a high IQ, such as money transfer, crafts, brokerage and so forth, ii) intelligence genes "stayed in the family" because of genetic isolation and higher reproductive fitness of well-to-do families, iii) the same or similar genes were in charge of genetic disorders; as a result, the latter were passed from generation to generation. Still, Cochran's team identified no genetic mechanism, which explicitly coupled a genetic disorder with high intelligence; their arguments are mostly circumstantial. Another weak point of the theory is its questionable completeness. For example, a rabbi raised the issue of the Christian tradition of celibacy of priests and monks. They were often exceptionally intelligent but were excluded from the reproductive process; this could further magnify the intellectual disparity. Cochran's study ignored this phenomenon.

It seems that Jews are far from being delighted by this recent study, which suggests that their phenomenal success in science and culture appears to merely be a consequence of the medieval discrimination hardwired in their genes, which was paid for by personal tragedies over many centuries. Though high intelligence of Ashkenazim may be of a mixed social-genetic origin, as this theory implies, it was really a result of the Covenant. It is because of their insistence on being the Chosen People, the Jews were discriminated against over a period of two millennia and this is also why they developed both a high IQ and hereditary diseases.

Spirituality: The God Gene

Jews in a Nazi death camp decide to put God on trial, they appoint a judge, prosecutor, and attorney, and hold prolonged deliberations, after which they sentence God to death for their sufferings; at this point a rabbi announces that the time has come for evening prayer. This story illustrates the intensity of the human need for spirituality and faith.

Human spirituality is one of those many things we know very little about, though nobody can doubt its incredible power. Anthropologists believe that images on walls of caves painted as early as thirty thousand years ago, which depict strange creatures with human bodies and animal heads, had to do with religious ceremonies. Thus, religion, which is one of the main forms of spirituality, has existed for many thousands of years. Surveys show that seventy percent of Americans believe in an afterlife and more than eighty percent believe in God. In Israel, as a recent poll shows, nearly seventy four percent believe in God. The intensity of religious senti-ments may reach the level of absurdity; that is why religious zealots have been responsible for some of the most outraged atrocities in the human history.

This world would look completely different without the human need for faith and the capacity for enlightenment. Meditation and creativity in arts such as music, painting, and acting may be accompanied by vivid spir-itual experiences. Rational thinking, the basis for exact sciences, is also tightly interwoven with spiritual motivation. The saying: "ideas govern the world" does not seem to be a gross exaggeration; ideas were behind crucial historic upheavals, wars, revolutions, and technological breakthroughs. Without religious taboos, like the prohibition of incest, humans would apparently disappear as a species. For an individual, spirituality seems to offer better chances in the struggle of physical and social survival, providing a sense of purpose, hope, and consistency. Indian spiritual practices known as yoga that originated thousands of years ago become more and more popular. Dietary limitations and systematical prayers stabilize heart-rate and benefit health in general.

Are we born with a need for spirituality? Instincts are unconscious reactions we perform without thinking or learning. They are innate. We are well familiar with instincts such as taking care of offspring, keeping equilibrium while walking or feeling attraction to the opposite gender with subsequent sexual excitement.

In a recent book, geneticist Dean Hamer promotes a theory that spirituality is innate and is therefore controlled by genes like a Mendelian trait. He argues that all people inherit this instinct to a certain degree. Given this assumption, we are left with a problem: is it possible to quantify spirituality? If this were the case, then one can measure spirituality of representative groups of a population, take their DNA samples and identify the genes in charge. To measure spirituality, Hamer employed the so-called *self-transcendence scale* developed by the psychologist Robert Cloninge; it characterizes a person's capacity to submerge himself in enlightenment, or "reaching out beyond himself/herself". Studies of identical and fraternal twins as well as a comparison between them and unrelated people have shown that spirituality, as defined by the above self-transcendence scale, can be inherited to a substantial degree.

Hamer claims to have identified a particular gene, referred to as the God gene, which encodes proteins called *monoamines* and controls brain signal activity. Monoamines include various substances, such as *dopamine*, a vital chemical, which is naturally released by the human body following pleasurable activities like food consumption or sex. Faulty dopamine production may bring about severe health problems. What is of particular interest in the present context is that cocaine and other drugs block a normal distribution of dopamine in a human body, altering consciousness and bringing about mystical sensations; therefore, dopamine plays a major role in narcotics addiction.

Hamer's theory poses more questions than answers and appears problematic. Take, for example, these two extremities: a pagan Malaysian sect worshipping a giant teapot, as was reported by media, and followers of a monotheistic religion like Judaism, Christianity, or Islam. Both of these groups may reach the same degree of "reaching out beyond himself/herself" or, to put it simply, Nirvana. They may therefore appear similar, if judged by the self-transcendence scale. Still, we feel there is something fundamentally wrong in this conclusion; in addition to the ability of "submerging in enlightenment", there should also be common sense and, at least, a bit of rationality. A man-made teapot, however big, just cannot be the all-mighty God. Moreover, as Hamer's gene and narcotics affect production of the same brain chemicals, it does not seem possible to distinguish the "enlightenment" due to the innate need for spirituality from that due to drugs, because the self-transcendence scale, the basis of Hamer's experiments, would show similar results.

Further, if Hamer's theory holds true, then Jews, who discovered the universal, all-mighty and unobservable God, should be genetically different from other people. In other words, Hamer's gene should manifest itself among the Jews in a particularly explicit way, and, if spirituality can be quantified with the help of this or that "scale", this difference can be recorded and verified. Are we at last close to deciphering the code of the Jewish singularity? This does not seem to be the case. As can be seen from the above considerations of "Jewish" genetics, there is no evidence whatsoever of a genetic disparity between Jews and gentiles.

3

Memes

I have found after all the books, cogitation, and self-absorption, a people without whom life would be intolerable.

—Nancy Yos, a convert of twenty seven.

The Idea as Virus

Though not of a genetic origin, the Jewish uniqueness is obviously an "inherited" trait and there should be a proper mechanism. Besides genes, assets, debts, etc., we definitely inherit other things The complete list of what we inherit also consists of ideas, traditions, and beliefs. That is why this chapter deals with the basic Jewish memes as the factors which have shaped the Jewish "otherness".

Humans have a soft spot for ideas that is both, a curse and a blessing, depending on the content of ideas and their implementation. Cultural and scientific themes had been around from ancient times, but their "inherited" nature remained implicit and vague. With the discovery of genes, it became possible to formulate a similar concept in the fields of science and culture, the so-called *memes*. These are scientific or cultural units transmitted among individuals via rituals, writings, equations, movies, speech, traditions, images, etc. To put it simply, a meme is a contagious idea, an ideological virus, and is intentionally named so as to rhyme with "gene". A gene is a product of nature; a meme is a product of nurture. Thus, religion, social ideas, literary heroes, inventions, the notion of democracy and a fashionable haircut are all examples of memes. There is absolutely no relevance attached to the content or meaning of the idea or image, its moral, social, historic or scientific value. What matters is only the meme's capacity of replicating and multiplying.

The term was coined by a biologist Richard Dawkins in 1976, though the analogy between an idea and a virus had been discussed by various authors much earlier. The notion of meme was derived as a by-product of Dawkins' concept of "the selfish gene", a gene which cares only about its own reproduction in complete disregard of what happens to its carrier. Dawkins interprets Darwin's evolution through survival of the fittest as survival of a "selfish gene". The same holds true for a meme, it is a "selfish meme", and it is concerned solely with its own survival.

The concept of the selfish gene met with opposition among geneticists because Dawkins had not pointed to a relevant genetic mechanism to support it; outside of explanations of human behavior, it remains largely useless. However, the notion of meme was indeed found to be convenient for discussions of various historical, religious and social issues in a unified framework.

There are also differences between the gene and the meme which are not difficult to identify. Though your genes are defined by your parents, your memes follow from the environment as well. Obviously, the command of language as well as available technological means, are critical for the capacity of a meme to copy itself. That is why memes are typical of human society, unlike genes, which are common to living creatures in general. Unlike genes, memes may be localized in both time and space. They may have an ethnic component: memes of a Brazilian tribe surviving in the Amazon jungles differ from those of the French. Yet another difference is the speed of multiplication: there is no limit for the memes, besides perhaps the technological one, however, a human female has a limited fertility age and cannot therefore give birth to more than approximately twenty children.

Most of us manage to make a leaving because of memes: teachers, clergy, fashion models, engineers, singers, clerks, and so forth. We refer to memes on a daily basis; those of us working in media, Internet, public relations and promotion agencies get paid for spreading memes. We are frequently told that the legal system exists for ensuring "justice for all". This

WRONG

Good example

is far from being the case, as this system is based on memes: laws, procedures, and verdicts, which is why it cares mainly about its own survival, its memes. Justice is served as a by-product, when it helps to replicate legal memes.

If humans are meme machines, then the Jews are probably the most productive of these: they have generated the most infectious and enduring ideas. The Jewish meme machine has worked continuously for around three or perhaps four millennia; it would be sufficient to invoke the comment of Malaysian's prime-minister Mohamed Mahathir once again: "They invented socialism, communism, human rights and democracy…". Characteristically, Mahathir, a devoted Muslim, forgot to mention that Jews "invented" the Muslim God.

Abraham was responsible for Jewish genes, he was also in charge of Arab genes, and thereby there is nothing racial in being a Jew. Jews are not a race as any convert of Asian or African origin can affirm. Jewish memes have their roots in Moses; anybody accepting the Law of Moses can become a Jew, regardless of his or her ethnic origins, in other words: *Jews prefer memes over genes*, pointing thereby to the very roots of the Jewish phenomenon.

The memes' world is a world in war; which is why memes vary, make alliances, mutate and copulate. Being a cause of social and technological changes, they may possess enormous power. Memes may be a matter of life or death, prosperity or bankruptcy. The Jewish and anti-Jewish memes considered in this chapter are the main factors which shaped the Jewish "otherness". Also, they are a good example of such a war. Though the memes below may appear as a somewhat kaleidoscopic collection, they make up the very fabric of the Jewish phenomenon.

Anti-Jewish Memes

Jews gave birth to two principal categories of memes: memes *of* Jews, Jewish memes, and memes *about* Jews, mostly being *anti*-Jewish memes. Some of the anti-Jewish memes appear dead, among them the belief that the Jews have tails, which miraculously disappear after conversion to Christianity. The memes of ritual murder and blood libel still survive, as illustrated by Beilis' affair and the meme of Judas Iscariot.

Since the Middle Ages, it has been the Catholic Church which periodically instigated these accusations; in the Beilis'case, they came from the rightist Russian Orthodoxy. In 1911, a poor Jewish inhabitant of Kiev, Mendel Beilis was arrested and accused of murdering a Christian boy, Andrei Yushinsky, as a part of his preparations for the upcoming Passover festivities. The case captured the attention of the media and was highly publicized. Soon it became clear that the government had nothing to substantiate the accusations and the jury, mostly Ukrainian peasants, unanimously declared Beilis not guilty. Amazingly, this did not kill the meme. Recently, bodies of several teenagers were found in the city of Krasnoyarsk, Siberia, to immediately reignite rumors of the Jewish soft spot for Christian blood as a component of their Passover bread.

The dogmatic image of Judas Iscariot betraying the Messiah for thirty pieces of silver and kissing him the notorious "kiss of Judas" is a classic Christian meme. The recently reconstructed Coptic text of the so-called *Gospel of Judas*, dating back to the third or fourth century, presents another story: Judas was not a traitor but an obedient disciple who followed Jesus' instructions to hand him over to the Romans. Because this or similar document was marked by the Bishop of Lyons, Irenaeus, as heresy in 189 C.E., it was condemned and banned by the Church. Indeed, from its very beginning, the Church, as other establishments, ruled through bureaucracy, including manipulations of religious memes, editing, approving, and prohibiting documents as it pleased. This produced at least two remarkable metamorphoses. From the earliest to the final version of the Gospels, Judas Iscariot, an observant Jew, had evolved from a vague apostle to the incarnation of evil, symbolizing the Jews, the treacherous maligning tribe. At the same time, Jesus, another observant Jew, nearly lost his ethnic identity, becoming purely the Son of God and Son of Man.

Another tenacious meme is the story of the Wandering Jew as a certain personality, which first appeared in Europe during the Dark Ages. The legend is that a Jew (or a Roman) who punched Jesus on his way to the Crucifixion was cursed to wander until the Second Coming of Christ. By one of the versions, a gate-keeper struck him and said in mockery, "Go quicker, Jesus; why do you loiter?" and Jesus looking back at him replied, "I am going, and you shall wait till I return". Over the centuries, there were people who claimed to have actually seen the Wandering Jew, who, in the meantime, had become the hero of several novels.

The enduring anti-Jewish meme is a claim that Jews always knew the truth about Jesus being the Son of God and the Messiah but deliberately rejected him. Therefore, they are not human but are followers of Satan. This theory was set forward by Pope Gregory the Great in the beginning of the Seventh century. It took the Catholic Church more than a millennium to change its mind: in 1965 the collective guilt of the Jews for the crucifixion of Jesus was lifted and, recently, John Paul II called the Jews "our elder brothers" and "people of the Covenant". Still, the meme is very much alive.

The theory of world domination is striving in a variety of versions. A new-born meme of this category claims that Jews planned the terror attack on the Twin Towers on September 11, 2001, and that, as a result, there were no Jewish victims; four thousand Jews employed there did not show up on that day. There are only two thousand Jews out of a population of four million and a half in the prosperous and carefree country of Norway. Still, a new mutation of this meme surfaced there in 2003: the Association of New Medicine announced that international Jewry had a cure for most lethal illnesses, including cancer, but kept the treatment secret in order to exterminate gentiles.

The Soviet era gave birth to a new meme of Birobidzhan. In 1928, in a challenge to both Zionism and Judaism, Stalin set up the Jewish Autonomous Region in swamplands of the Siberian Far East, near the border with China, known as Birobidzhan. Characteristically, Yiddish, not Hebrew, was defined as the official language. Stalin obviously had in mind to distance Jews from central, politically sensitive areas of the Soviet Union. Later, in 1953, when the "Doctors' Plot" triggered the anti-Semitic campaign, Jews were preparing to be deported to this region. Ecology made living conditions there extremely harsh, though idealistic Jews began to settle there. Promoting this initiative, the government even produced a cute but cooked movie named *"Seekers of Happiness"* about a Jewish family leaving the United States for Birobidzhan to build a new life; in another case, a plane dropped propaganda leaflets over a shtetel in Byelorussia.

Overall, this project was a complete failure as it never appealed to the Jewish masses with their immediate physical roots in Ukraine, Byelorussia, or Russia, and their spiritual heritage in Canaan. In 1998, the total population consisted of two hundred thousand people, of which only two percent was Jewish. As I noted earlier, this meme, almost unknown outside of the Soviet Union, infected a famous gentile mathematician, John Nash, the Nobel Prize winner and a mental patient, in a mysterious way. Nash was suffering from schizophrenia and hallucinating, among other things, about Birobidzhan.

Another anti-Jewish meme, a mutation of the ancient Greek myth of Atlantis, followed from a fundamental effort of various racist movements, the Nazis in particular, to replace Judaism and Christianity with their own spirituality. The most they were capable of was an attempt at modifying old pagan myths and ceremonies. This story is really dramatic and deserves separate considerations.

Atlantis, Shamballa, and Wewelsburg Castle

Plato had apparently noble intentions when nearly two thousand years ago, he told the world about a terrific island populated by demigods which was then forgotten somewhere in the ocean. With the rise of the Nazis, this innocent meme of the lost civilization of Atlantis, a product of the ancient Greek culture, had developed virulent anti-Jewish mutations.

Approximately eleven thousand years ago, there was an island called Atlantis situated somewhere in the Atlantic Ocean and inhabited by a mighty, prosperous race. Its people were engaged in agriculture and trade and reached as far as Europe and Africa. Poseidon, the god of the sea, fell in love with Atlantis' woman, Cleito, who gave birth to his sons: five sets of twins. These became rulers of Atlantis, with the island divided among the brothers. Atlas was the first King. Temple of Poseidon, the god of the sea, with his huge gold statue riding on a chariot, dominated the center of Atlantis. The island also featured dwellings, moats, canals, lakes, and mountains. Fertile soil and the climate allowed for two harvests a year. Animals, herbs, fruits, and nuts were in abundance. Plato provided figures concerning the sizes of ditches, bridges, and even data about Atlantis' mighty military. This paradise could not last forever. Soon corruption became widespread among Atlanteans, spurring the fury of Zeus. His retaliation was swift and lethal: in one wild heave, the island was swallowed by the ocean.

Plato's captivating story prompted much interest and controversy over the period of nearly two thousand years, inspiring novelists, musicians, and movie makers. Jules Verne's hero, Captain Nemo, visited the submerged island on the board of his submarine, Nautilus. It is the actual location of Atlantis which became a subject of dispute. According to one version, Atlantis was located in the Azores Islands some nine hundred miles west of the Portuguese coast. Another theory claimed that the volcanic island of Thera near Crete in the Aegean Sea was Atlantis, as in approximately 1,500 B.C.E. this island was blasted by a volcanic eruption. A recent theory was proposed by a Russian enthusiast, Viatcheslav Koudriavtsev: Atlantis was located on the Celtic Shelf around England, the area which, during the last Ice Age over ten thousand years ago, was above the water.

This charming pagan meme had been free of any anti-Jewish overtones for nearly two thousand years, until the rise of the Nazis changed its very meaning. One of the German reactions to the catastrophe of the First World War was increased popularity of neo-pagan teachings, of which the *Thule-* and *Vril-*societies were the most prominent promoters. Their agenda professed the destruction of the Roman Empire by pagan Teutonic tribes as a crucial sign of Teutonic superiority. It was Hitler who realized that this argument was problematic: "...Romans were erecting great buildings, when our forefathers were living in mud huts". If he had been sharp enough to overcome his obsessions, go on along this line and notice, as Disraeli, Twain, and Churchill did, that Jews had created the great civilization and wrote the Bible when the Roman Empire did not yet even exist, then perhaps, the Second World War and the Holocaust would never have happened. However, Hitler was controlled by his fixations rather than by rational thinking. The Nazis mistook the theory of German transcendence for a scientific fact, which implied that the German race should be granted special rights. The Jewish civilization, which had deprived the Germans of their superiority, should be destroyed at any cost. Christianity, as post-Judaism, could hardly be tolerated.

The members of Thule speculated that the Teutonic tribesmen had their origins from Iceland or Greenland, and ultimately came from the lost kingdom of Atlantis. The Nazi racial expert, Alfred Rosenberg, wrote about a "Nordic-Atlantean" master race in *The Myth of the Twentieth Century*". Another fashionable teaching, promoted by a founder of Vril, Karl Haushofer, was Buddhism with its elite form practiced in Tibet; there were speculations that the latter was also somehow connected with Atlantis. Hitler, who was personally familiar with Haushofer, saw in mysticism, and Buddhism in particular, a way of creating a New World free of the Jews. A race of supermen and demigods could be reborn, if the secrets of Atlantis and Tibet were discovered.

The Nazi desire to cover up the destruction of European Jewry with a "scientific and objective" justification produced one surprising result. The Jewish Museum in Prague presently contains one of the richest collections of Judaica; in a paradoxical way, it survived the war thanks to Hitler. When amidst the Holocaust, leaders of Czech Jewry approached the Nazis with the idea of preserving Jewish artifacts in a special museum, Hitler enthusiastically supported it and even proposed the name: "Museum of Extinct Race". This was meant to let anybody to see the degenerative Jewish culture.

The Nazis thus pursued a two-track policy: the first stage was the total elimination of Jews responsible for the corrupt world order, followed by the second stage, the rebirth of a pure White Race, which was to fill the vacuum and thereby create a New World. Heinrich Himmler, who once made his living as a chicken farmer, was responsible for both sides of the coin and began to think of himself as the reincarnation of King Heinrich I, founder of the first German Reich. He set out on a campaign of transforming the SS-troops, originally Hitler's bodyguards, into a sort of Aryan knighthood. Its headquarters were situated in the medieval Wewelsburg Castle, twelve miles south-west of Paderborn. It had been rented by Himmler in 1934 for one Reichsmark per year for a period of one hundred years. The latter figure shows how over-optimistic the Nazi leaders were in those times.

Wewelsburg became a neo-pagan Temple of the "noble soul and blood", the incubator of a White superman, *Ubermensch*, and of the Aryan religion, in a direct showdown with Christianity. In a paradoxical way, it was the Church which used the castle during the seventeenth century to torture and execute prisoners accused of witchery; tens of thousands of "witches" met their painful death there. Thus, Himmler skillfully selected the right place for his occult rituals. This venue was to evolve to a sort of seat of a knightly order and become the spiritual focus of the Aryan world. The castle also hosted wedding ceremonies for the SS officers over which Himmler often presided. It also served as a depository for Death's Head rings of the SS which were granted after three years of outstanding military service and, in case of death, stored again at the castle.

German academics readily participated in this pagan drive, providing scientific basis and documentation. In 1935, Himmler established the Ancestral Heritage Society, *Das Ahnenerbe*, which served as the SS-arm, staffed with professors and experts in archeology, anthropology and related fields, all of whom had been recruited into the SS. It was meant to find roots of the Aryan race and thus provide a foundation for the theory of the innate superiority of the German people, with the help of anthropological and archaeological evidence. Its members undertook expeditions around the world, to the Canary Islands in search of Atlantis, to Iceland in search of the Holy Grail and even to Iran for possible extant certificates of Aryan kings.

A special place was reserved for Tibet and Buddhism. There, on the roof of the world, safely hidden behind Tibetan snow peaks, lies the mystical kingdom of *Shamballa*, as local monks are convinced. Shamballa is ruled by enlightened kings guarding the secret commandments of Buddhism; in the future, a king of Shamballa would lead his great army to exterminate all the dark forces of evil, and the world would become the place of wisdom, peace, and happiness. In 1937, a special lecture was given to a selected group of SS-troops about the similarity between teachings of the Führer and those of "the other great Aryan personality, the Buddha". In 1938, Himmler sent a well-equipped expedition to Tibet headed by Ernst Schaefer, a sort of German Indiana Jones, and anthropologist Bruno Beger. The latter, who believed that the shape of the skull controlled the moral and intellectual capacities of an individual, took measurements of hundreds of local tribesmen in search of a possible Aryan ancestry. With the outbreak of the war, the Society became involved in looting European and Russian museums and collections, shipping the trophies to the Wewelsburg Castle, to Berlin, or just presenting them to high-ranking Nazis.

As a man of deeds, Himmler understood that the memes being dealt with at Wewelsburg would not suffice; he had to take care of the genes too. To this end, in 1935, he started the *Lebensborn* project of clandestine breeding of Aryan human beings. Do not make a mistake, it was indeed meant to literally arrange copulation of a "racially valuable" male, mostly from the SS-troops, and a "racially valuable" female, mainly from Germany or Norway. Then the Lebensborn project would take care of the offspring. This would greatly improve the genetic pool of the Master Race and would thereby provide the Führer with superior soldiers. Medical staff, housing, and finances were no problem.

There were hundreds of thousands of the German troops stationed in Norway during the war, all in impressive uniforms, and plenty of nice Norwegian girls, thirsty for love and affection. They could not care less about racial purity, but the stage was set for a giant experiment in Eugenics. With rare exception, the Norwegian people treated the girls as "German whores" and the results of the experiment were mostly tragic. Following the war, the girls were ostracized and persecuted; the Norwegian government went so far as to appoint a psychiatric expert for examining the children. This was in fact a racist move in the opposite direction: the children were suspected of having deficient German genes.

A key activist of the Ancestral Heritage Society, skull's collector, Wolfram Sievers, was put on trial at Nuremberg after the war, found guilty and hanged for experiments with inmates of the death camps. However, other members escaped punishment and enjoyed the status of respected scientists.

Haushofer, mentioned earlier, an eccentric personality, was a rare combination of professional soldier and expert on Geopolitics and Oriental mysticism. He became an enthusiastic follower of esoteric teachings during his stay in Japan in 1908 as an artillery instructor. He then traveled in the Far East, including India and Tibet, and managed to acquire fluent Korean, Japanese, Hindu, and Chinese; he also spoke French, English, and Russian. Haushofer influenced Hitler's policy of expansion via his connections with high-ranking Nazis and was a key figure behind special relations between Japan and Germany. He also formed a viewpoint of the SS as a German adaptation of the Japanese Samurai. Ironically, his wife was half-Jewish, which according to the racial decrees, made her fully Jewish; Haushofer was to resort to his close relations with Rudolph Hess, Hitler's deputy, who provided a special certificate granting Frau Haushofer the status of "honorable German". But the tragedies were waiting. Their son Albrecht, a geography expert and a poet, was executed by the Gestapo in 1944 for participation in a plot to assassinate Hitler. After the war, Haushofer was interrogated by the Allies for his part in war crimes and released. In 1946, he and his wife committed suicide by drinking poison; Haushofer, as a devoted Samurai, did not miss this occasion of performing the Japanese ritual of *hara-kiri*. In taking their own lives, they merely followed their bosses.

Indeed, in the last days of the war, suicide became a popular Nazi ceremony. Joseph Goebbels, the main Nazi manipulator of public opinion, and his wife did it on a monumental scale: they first poisoned their six children and then committed suicide. The "just married" couple, Adolph Hitler and Eva Braun, also killed themselves. Apparently, Hitler needed a shock of the upcoming self-destruction to display any affection for his long-time intimate companion and arranged a wedding ceremony hours prior to the suicide. The strained groom managed at last to publicly kiss his permanently depressed bride on the lips but failed to control chaotic tremors of his left hand. Making his disappearance from this world as complete as possible, he arranged the destruction of his favorite Alsatian dog, Blondi, and all of her puppies. The self-annihilations were a culmination of the pagan cult these Nazis worshipped; they left no offspring. What a loss for the Aryan genetic pool!

Towards the end of the war, Himmler betrayed his Führer by trying to negotiate the German surrender with the Allies and then, captured by the British, poisoned himself. But in the late thirties, he had been planning a great future for his Temple. Since 1940, Wewelsburg had been under renovation by inmates of a concentration camp, especially built for this purpose nearby. More than one thousand prisoners, a third, died in the process. The plans were doomed, as it soon became clear that Germany was not going to win the war. In 1945, a special SS-unit, hand-picked by Himmler, blew up the entire complex behind the front line of the advancing American troops; then it took Germany thirty four years to rebuild it as a historic site.

The primitive Nazi efforts of merging the ancient pagan myths with the groundless speculations regarding innate German superiority could not meet the minimal criteria of common sense. Nazi leaders, who wisely exploited the darkest human instincts and assembled sophisticated war machinery, failed to develop any reasonable alternative to Judaism and its two offshoots.

From God to the Messiah

The ferocity of the above anti-Jewish memes and severity of their consequences are unparallel. Yet, from a historic point of view they are transients. There must be something in the Jewish memes that penetrates the very soul of a human being and keeps adhered. Judaism and its two offshoots endure because they touch on the essence of human nature.

One of the Israeli prisons, Megiddo, is situated near Armageddon, the Biblical site of a future decisive showdown between good and evil. Recently, its inmates, mostly common criminals, have been employed in renovation works. They developed interest in archeology because of the discovery made within the prison's walls: excavations of the courtyard unraveled ruins of a church dating back to the third or fourth century and thought to be among the oldest in the world. The key finding was a well-preserved mosaic bearing the name of Jesus and referring to him as God. With this discovery, the inmates touched on the very core of Jewish spirituality: the meme of God, which is the greatest of the Jewish memes, and the meme of Messiah.

The omnipotent, all-mighty God was not a part of the world and was not amenable to human understanding. On the contrary, the world was merely his creation; history itself was made by God. Any attempt to scientifically prove or disapprove God's existence was therefore doomed from the very beginning. Maimonides (Rambam) comments that God is Eternal, above time and beyond space. God cannot be born and cannot die. The attempts of simulating Him or believing in other gods are sinful and contemptuous.

God of the Jews was a merciless God. Abraham's loyalty was tested in a particularly cruel way by ordering him to kill his son, Isaac; a subsequent nullification of the command does not seem to justify its severity. After departure from Egypt, the tribe was ordered to wander for forty-years in the harsh Sinai desert. Moses, the great lawgiver and father of the nation, was not allowed to enter the Land of Israel, his life-time venture, and his burial site remains unknown. God instructs the Israelites about their attitude towards the pagan Canaanites: "You shall tear down their altars and break their pillars". In case of adultery, both a wife and her lover must be put to death, and so forth.

The Jewish God was also a merciful God, prohibiting sadistic physical punishments popular among other nations, like castration, facial mutilation, and flogging to death. He was fair: human life is sacred; crimes of the parents must not be avenged by execution of their children; the wife of a criminal must not be forced into prostitution, and so forth.

The notion of God has not changed since its discovery (some would say creation) by the ancient Hebrews nearly three millennia ago. The Jewish God also became the Christian and the Muslim God. Because of the inherent combination of both universality and simplicity, this notion seems to be the highest epitome of what the human imagination is capable of. It is a remarkably stable and coherent meme, which may well survive as long as mankind does. Yet, there is a fundamental difficulty with the circumstances surrounding the birth of this meme: no rational explanations of this spiritual breakthrough, the giant leap from worshipping hand-made and narrowly specialized idols to the concept of a Jewish God, are available as yet. We are left with a difficult choice: either to accept the Biblical story of Divine intervention or reject it; in the latter case, no reasonable narrative exists that is capable of competing with the Bible.

The Old Testament, written around the middle of the first millennia B.C.E., also contains other powerful Jewish ideas attributed mainly to Moses, and later adopted by Christianity and Islam. First of all, there are the Ten Commandments, or the Decalogue, the simplest version of which is as follows: "I am YHWH your God; You shall have no other gods besides me; You shall not make yourselves a graven image; You shall not take the name of YHWH in vain; Remember the Sabbath day; Honor your father and mother; You shall not kill; You shall not commit adultery; You shall not steal; You shall not bear false witness; You shall not covet".

The Mosaic covenant thus was put in a definitive legal framework, which was a major step toward a civilized society as we understand it today. It was also unique in being the treaty between God and people, not between two states or a state and people. God was recognized by the Jews as the ultimate and totalitarian ruler controlling every aspect of daily human behavior. There was no distinction between the religious and the secular, as Moses acted as both the prophet and the lawgiver. This was to have far-reaching consequences; in particular, it paved way for religious fanaticism, which later spilled over into Christianity and Islam. This also encouraged the Jewish tendency towards rebellion: if God is the ultimate sovereign, who needs mortal government officials? In fact, Judaism began from a rebellion against idolatry. The Exodus was another powerful manifestation of this mentality, which Jeremiah noted back in 627 B.C.E.: "This people hath a revolting and rebellious heart".

The Covenant treated all the Israelites, the rich and the poor, equally. It included, for example, explicit and strict limitations on sexual activity, absolutely banning adultery, homosexuality, and bestiality. One gets the impression that the ancient Israelites knew something about Mendelian genes: they prohibited incest.

Unlike the meme of God, that of the Messiah underwent significant mutation from the time of its birth in sacred Jewish scripts more than two millennia ago. The very word originated from "*Mashiach*", in Hebrew, which simply means "anointed to serve God". The Israelites used to anoint their Kings and High Priests with oil. The Greek word "*Christ*" is a literal translation of "*Mashiach*". The concept itself appeared in prophecies of Hosea, Ezekiel, Jeremiah, and Isaiah: "The wolf shall dwell with the lamb, the leopard shall lie down with the kid". This was the belief in a perfect world of perfect harmony, which would materialize under specified conditions. Many of these prophecies pointed to a descendant of King David as Messiah. The Jewish Messiah is a man, like Moses, and is second to him. The coming of Messiah should include gathering of all the Jews in the Land of Israel and building the Third Temple. Moreover, "God will be King over all the world on that day, God will be One and His Name will be One" and "Nation shall not lift up sword against nation, neither shall man learn war anymore".

Bar Kochba, Shabettai Zevi and others declared themselves as Messiah but failed miserably. A recent case involved Menachem Mendel Schneerson, the late leader of the Chabad Hasidic sect, who was believed by his followers to be the Messiah though he had not stated that. After his death in 1994, these zealots expected his reappearance.

Jesus obviously could not comply with the above attributes of the Jewish Messiah. In particular, he was Son of God and Son of Man at the same time; he could not prove that there was a trace of David's genes in his blood; he also failed to restore the Kingdom, as the Messiah was supposed to do. Christian claims that the perfect world would be materialized upon the Second Coming were rejected in that the very idea is foreign to Judaism. Jesus therefore could not be the Jewish Messiah. Islam offered yet another view of Jesus, (Isa in the Koran): he was a mortal human but a prophet. He was not crucified but raised to heaven to come back at the end of days for the rest of his natural life; he would be preceded by another personality, Mahdi, and both of them would fight evil in the world.

The vast majority of prophets known to mankind were Jewish. Judaism was always aware of the fact that the dividing line between being a saint and being insane is very thin. Some of the biblical prophets indeed behaved or at least appeared as *meshuga*, the Hebrew word for "crazy". It is well known that mental patients, schizophrenics in particular, may tend to think of themselves as the Messiah or, at least, as prophets. According to the Jewish Oral Law formalized in the *Talmud*, no prophesying was possible from the destruction of the Second Temple onwards, the rule which was designed to specifically protect Judaism from fraudulent prophets. Furthermore, Maimonides, a prominent physician of his time, formulated rules by which a genuine prophet should be judged: a sharp intellect and a coherent response to his environment.

The Hebrew tradition of circumcision can be traced back to Abraham's times. Hebrews believed it had certain medical benefits, reducing the chance of venereal disease, urinary tract infections, and so forth. Indeed, recent studies by French and South African researchers suggest that circumcision reduces the risk of HIV infection by as much as sixty percent. The ancient Egyptians, Edomites, Ammonites, and Moabites also practiced circumcision but performed it around the age of thirteen, the age of male puberty. Only Hebrews attached a transcendental meaning to this custom, symbolizing unity with the Chosen People. The circumcision was performed as a special ceremony on the eighth day after birth.

Sometimes, one may take advantage of circumcision in a most unusual way. The Biblical story has it that the Jewish woman Dinah was raped by Schechem, son of a Canaanite chieftain, on her way to see friends. Unexpectedly, the rapist fell in love with his victim and approached her family with a proposition of marriage; he further claimed that Canaanites and Hebrews should intermarry to end the animosity between the two peoples. Dinah's brothers replied that, as Canaanites did not practice circumcision, marrying them would be intolerably sinful for Hebrew women. They also stated that there would be no problem if Schechem and his kinsmen would undergo circumcision. Once the Canaanites underwent this painful operation and were temporarily disabled, the brothers killed all of them. Embracing foreign memes, it turns out, should be accompanied with necessary precautions.

Yom Kippur or the Day of Atonement is the last of the *Ten Days of Repentance* and thought of as the most sacred day of the year. Fasting, the total abstention from all food and drink, starts before sundown and ends after nightfall the following day. At this day, God makes his decision concerning every Jew: "those that are found worthy by God are said to be written in the Book of Life". This is the origin of the popular greeting "May you be inscribed". In order to signify their purity from sins, Jews wear white clothing on this day.

A little known but tenacious meme of *Pulsa d'Nura*, which may be translated from Aramaic as "whip of fire", is a controversial semi-pagan ceremony of cursing somebody to death. The subject of the curse has to be a sinner of proper magnitude to merit such intensive care. Because of the severity of a desirable outcome, performers of the ceremony usually keep the details for themselves. One of the options is a night gathering of rabbis and religious zealots at a cemetery and common prayer to God or to angels of destruction to refrain from forgiving the sinful subject and kill him within a year or even immediately.

Amazingly, this black magic appears to work. The highly-publicized "successful" cases of enacting Pulsa d'Nura involved late Yitzhak Rabin who was blamed for his attempts of implementing the Oslo Accords and, more recently, Ariel Sharon for transferring territories adjacent to Gaza to Palestinian control.

Main-stream rabbis claim that Pulsa d'Nura cannot be a part of Judaism. Rabbi Ariel Bar Tzadok explained why: "the only way a Jew is put to death is for violation of specific Biblical laws and then only after being tried and condemned by a kosher and authoritative Sanhedrin, the likes of which have not existed in Israel and among the Jewish people since the days of the Temple".

Muhammad the Wolf and Jewish Scriptures

Scholars believe that the Torah was put *into writing* as far back as the fourth century B.C.E. As the originals had been lost, any attempt to address the historical validity of the Torah was a formidable task. Thanks to a Bedouin shepherd, the breakthrough came in the late forties with the discovery of the Qumran scrolls.

For a few millennia, Bedouins were desert dwellers, herding goats, camels, and sheep, and seasonally moving in search of grazing lands. They were known for their ferocious resistance to foreign cultures and their skills in breeding and riding highly prized Arabic horses. Traditionally, Bedouins, who populated huge areas from the Arabian Desert to the Negev, Sinai, and the Western Desert to the Sahara, were divided into tribes, each led by a sheikh. From the end of the fifties, many were forced to abandon their nomadic life and the Bedouin population started to decrease. Bedouins are still surrounded by an exotic halo; I knew a Jewish woman who was married three times, each time to a Bedouin.

In the spring of 1947, a group of Bedouins was looking after their flocks near the wadi (valley) Qumran, northwest of the Dead Sea, near the remnants of the ancient settlement of Qumran. The area is some twelve miles east of Jerusalem. When one of them tossed a rock into a cave trying to attract attention of a wandering goat, they heard a sound of smashing pottery. One of the Bedouins, Muhammad edh-Dhib, Muhammad the Wolf in Arabic, was curious and bold enough to return to the site after a few days and climb down into the cave. He found ten clay jars there, each of approximately twenty four inches in height, two of which contained parchment scrolls wrapped in linen. Through this find, Muhammad had set up a chain of events destined to change our understanding of Jewish history and monotheism. Although as early as the third century C.E. there had been rumors of ancient manuscripts found near Jericho, no single case had been documented. It took Muhammad the Wolf to discover ancient copies of the Book of Isaiah, collections of psalms, hymns, narratives of the Book of Genesis, and commentaries.

Via an antiquities dealer and after secret negations, scrolls were bought by Athanasius Yeshua Samuel, head (Metropolitan) of the Syrian Orthodox Church at St. Mark's Monastery in Jerusalem. Some of them ended up in the hands of Eleazar Sukenik of the Hebrew University in Jerusalem. Interestingly, the latter bought his scrolls from a dealer on November 29, 1947, the day of the United Nations resolution to establish the State of Israel. It was Sukenik who fully realized the historical value and religious magnitude of the discovery of the scrolls. Though search of numerous caves of Qumran for additional manuscripts was hindered by the undergoing Arab-Israeli war, on April 11, 1948, the American School of Oriental Research in Jerusalem released an announcement regarding the discovery of the St. Mark's collection; two weeks later, Sukenik made a statement about his scrolls.

"THE FOUR DEAD SEA SCROLLS Biblical Manuscripts dating back to at least 200 b.c. are for sale. This would be an ideal gift to an educational or religious institution by an individual or group. Box F 206". This was the text of the advertisement which appeared in the June issue of the *Wall Street Journal* in 1954 under the category of "Miscellaneous for Sale". The person behind this amazing ad was Metropolitan Samuel who, by that time, had moved to the United States. By a strange coincidence, Yigael Yadin, Sukenik's son and the second Chief of Staff of the Israel Defense Forces (IDF), was touring the United States and became aware of the ad. After clandestine negotiations in the style of Hollywood thrillers, Yadin purchased the scrolls for $250,000 on behalf of Israel. It was a good deal for Metropolitan Samuel who purchased them for a sum equivalent to $100. The Hashemite Kingdom of Jordan theoretically could sue for the scrolls, which were discovered in what was then its territory. This would however entail recognition of the Jewish state, something unthinkable during those times. All seven manuscripts are presently displayed in the Shrine of the Book which was especially constructed for this purpose in Jerusalem as a part of the Israel Museum.

Subsequent excavations, from 1949 to 1956, revealed that real treasures had been stored in eleven caves and the ruins of the Qumran settlement. A system of notation was devised to refer to a particular manuscript or fragment based on the number of the cave it was found in. Bedouins discovered the richest depositories of documents in three caves; archaeologists located the other caves. Altogether, fifteen thousand fragments of more than five hundred manuscripts were found written mainly in Hebrew and Aramaic. The scrolls were made primarily of animal skin and papyrus and written from right to left with a carbon-based ink.

Overall, the scrolls contained the complete and oldest texts of the Bible yet seen except for the Book of Esther. All were remarkably close to its medieval versions from which the standard King James Bible had been translated in the seventeenth century. Additional prophecies of Ezekiel, Jeremiah, and Daniel, which do not appear in the Bible, were also discovered. There were formulations of communal rules, regulations concerning conduct in war, psalms, and hymns. One of the caves produced a spectacular and intriguing piece of archeology: the scroll made of copper with a list of sixty-four underground hiding places, somewhere in the Land of Israel, containing caches of weapons, gold, silver, and manuscripts, as yet to be found. This scroll is presently housed in the Amman Archaeological Museum in Jordan. Scientists are convinced that the scrolls were a part of the library of a Jewish sect and were hidden away in the caves from the Romans at the very outbreak of the First Revolt, 66–70 C.E.

Remnants of the complex adjacent to the caves reveal sophisticated engineering skills, especially its gravity-flow aqueduct, which carried fresh water from surrounding cliffs to cisterns, pool, and ritual baths. There was a fortified tower and a special chamber, presumably utilized for writing scribes, a sort of an ancient office. The structure included a large dining hall, which also served as a place for communal gatherings. Great importance was attached to common meals, as can be seen from the following passage in the *Rule of Community*: "They shall eat in common and pray in common and deliberate in common. Wherever there are ten men of the Council of the Community there shall not lack a Priest among them. And they shall sit before him according to their rank and shall be asked their counsel in all things in that order. And when the table has been prepared for eating, and the new wine for drinking, the Priest shall be the first to stretch out his hand to bless the first fruits of the bread and new wine".

Carbon dating established that most of the documents were written between the middle of the second century B.C.E. and the first century

C.E.; there is only one Hebrew document from those dates: the Nash Papyrus of Egypt containing the text of the Ten Commandments. That is why the Qumran Scrolls are at focus of much attention and, consequently, controversy. There were even allegations that the Vatican tried to prevent the publication of the Scrolls because they contained a stricter version of Christianity than that given in the New Testament and makes the latter questionable. Some of the speculations were fairly bizarre, including a theory claiming that the scrolls were of extra-terrestrial origin.

Who were the men of Qumran? We know that the *Pharisees* were strict followers of the Torah, but democratic and popular. Their traditional opponents, the *Sadducees*, were conservative and noble monarchists; the *Sicarii* were militants, specializing in war against the Romans and their supporters. Still, the Qumran community had a special nuance. Some of the texts dealt with a conflict between the "Sons of Light", "the poor", led by a priest called the "Teacher of Righteousness" and their enemies, called the "Sons of Darkness". Sukenik set forth a theory that the scrolls had been written by the *Essens*, a sect of Messianic, ascetic, and apocalyptic Jews, rigorous followers of the Torah. Later, this theory was modified so as to imply that Qumran's inhabitants preached an early version of Christianity. Still, none of the scrolls mentioned the Son of God or his followers in any way. One can only wonder: how such a tiny nation could give birth to so many competing ideological streams at such an early stage of human history. Jews have maintained their tradition of splitting up into a variety of political parties until today. It appears that this traditional national attitude also contributed to the Jewish uniqueness.

As to the Essens, this is how Pliny, the Roman historian, described them: "On the west side of the Dead Sea, but out of range of the noxious exhalations of the coast, is the solitary tribe of the Essenes, which is remarkable beyond all other tribes in the whole world, as it has renounced all sexual desire, has no money, and has only palm-trees for company. Day by day the throng of refugees is recruited to an equal number by numerous accessions of persons tired of life and driven thither by waves of fortune to adopt their manners....Lying below the Essenes was formerly the town of

Engedi, second only to Jerusalem in the fertility of its land and in its groves of palm-trees but now like Jerusalem a heap of ashes.".

I can only substantiate this passage by noting that Ein-Gedi is presently a kibbutz situated on the cliffs near the Dead Sea. Its unique Botanical Garden includes, among others, African myrrh, mentioned in Solomon's *Song of Songs*; but the persimmon trees grown in the area in ancient times to extract their rich, luxurious perfume were irreversibly lost.

Big Bang and Jewish Tuxedo

The endless list of controversies that Jews were involved over the centuries contains one of literally cosmic proportions because it deals with the origins of the universe. There are tens of thousands of books concerned with this subject in MIT's Hayden library alone. By way of contrast, the Bible does the same in a few pages.

In his book, Simon Singh discussed various pagan myths of creation. The Chinese legend had it that Phan Ku the Giant Creator hatched from an egg and then used a chisel to cut up the earth's landscape; he then set the Sun, Moon and stars. He died after completing this task, which made it possible for his skull to form the dome of sky and his flesh, the soil; his blood became seas and rivers and his bones became rocks. Greeks were the first to encourage disputes on the structure of the universe and introduce mathematical methods to improve its understanding. Plato and Aristotle claimed that the universe was eternal, there had been no beginning.

The Biblical version once again contradicted the Greek traditions: the universe was God's creation, and, more precisely, a six-day creation. This principle was unexpectedly confirmed by science; astronomers are presently convinced that there was a sudden beginning to the world, the kickoff.

Einstein's theory of gravitation implied that there was a moment of creation, later referred to as the Big Bang. American astronomer Edwin Hubble observed that the velocity of a galaxy is proportional to its distance, which meant, when taken with other observations, that the universe was expanding. In 1948, George Gamow and Ralph Apher published a key paper presenting a mathematical analysis of the Big Bang for the first time. The model was enthusiastically embraced by the Catholic Church. In 1951, Pius XII, silent during the Holocaust, let himself go, addressing the Pontifical Academy of Science with an eloquent and bold lecture entitled "*The Proofs for the Existence of God in the Light of Modern Natural Science*". He stated that "...everything seems to indicate that the material universe had a mighty beginning in time, endowed as it was with vast reserves of energy, in virtue of which, at first rapidly and then ever more slowly, it evolved into its present state...". Pius XII went on with a passion of a professional artist: "In fact, it would seem that present-day science, with one sweeping step back across millions of centuries, has succeeded in bearing witness to that primordial *Fiat lux* uttered at the moment when, along with matter, there burst forth from nothing a sea of light and radiation, when the particles of chemical elements split and formed into millions of galaxies". He did not care to mention that this was the Jewish meme he had in mind.

Thus, religion and science were suddenly overlapping. It was a rare case of a junction of a theory of physicists, most of them atheists, with the teaching of the Church, adapted from the Jewish scriptures. As in the case of genetics, the Soviets merely banned the Big Bang model, with a party boss declaring that "falsifiers of science want to revive the fairy tale of the origin of the world from nothing"; only the Party knew the truth about the universe. By a typical Soviet method of resolving scientific disputes, followers of the Big Bang theory were sent to labor camps, and one of them, Matvei Bronstein, was shot as a "spy".

Still, the theory lacked experimental evidence. In 1964, the two radio-astronomers, Arno Penzias and Robert Wilson, discovered by chance a noise of extra-terrestrial origin, the so-called *cosmic background radiation* (CMB), which seemed to come from all directions. The scientists concluded that the noise was the echo of a huge explosion, the Big Bang. The burst was not confined to a particular region, but was an event, which simultaneously involved the entire finite universe; it was explosion of space "within itself". Penzias described this in the following charming way: "When you go out and you take your hat off, you are getting a little bit of warmth from the Big Bang right on your scalp". Computations showed that the Big Bang took place about fifteen billion years ago; this is due to enormous dimensions of the universe, which contains nearly one hundred billion galaxies each composed of one hundred billion stars.

When put in Biblical context, the Big Bang theory has to do with the Six Days of Creation. At the time of the discovery, the media exploded with the headline: "The Bible was right". There was, however, a fundamental difficulty. Scientific evidence, as noted earlier, indicated that the universe was roughly fifteen billion years old. This contradicted the Biblical age which could be calculated by summing up the generations mentioned in the Bible since Adam *plus* Six Days of Creation and which indicated that the universe was about five thousand seven hundred years old.

Can this contradiction be resolved? Gerald Schroeder, a Biblical expert, thinks that it is possible. The Bible draws a clear distinction between the age of mankind and that of the universe. Indeed, a Six Day Creation was a masterpiece; it was human history that started from Day Seven, which rapidly went wrong. The Jewish New Year, (see Appendix A), marked by blowing the *shofar*, commemorates initiation of the human soul, the soul of Adam, and the beginning of human history. Schroeder argues that the very concept of "time" during the Six Days of Creation is different; it should not be measured by our standard clock, as the sun is mentioned only on Day Four. That is why the notions of "day", "morning", or "evening", as far as we speak of the Six Days of Creation, are not well-defined.

One of the first kabalists, Nachmanides, taught as early as the thirteenth century that "time" was created on Day One together with the first substance. Remarkably, almost seven hundred years later, Einstein proposed his Theory of Relativity, which mathematically united space, time, and matter in a single triad with its components in mutual dependence. Einstein showed that time is not absolute; it depends on gravity and velocity. A few years on one planet may amount to several minutes on another. Here a clock may show fifteen billion years but there another clock may register only six days. The situation becomes even more complicated, if we take into account the fact that our universe is expanding; its size is increasing. Schroeder argues that following these lines it is possible to show that the Six Days of the Bible are, in fact, fifteen billion years, as predicted by science.

Yet, this mixture of religion and science seems problematic. In a recent article, Eric Cornell, who won the Nobel Prize in Physics in 2001, considers the Biblical version of creation, the so-called "intelligent design", versus evolution theory. He writes: "Should scientists, as humans, make judgments on...religion? Absolutely. Should we act on these judgments, in an effort to do good? You bet....Just do not claim that your science tells you..."what is God".... Stick with the plainest truth: science says nothing about intelligent design, and intelligent design brings nothing to science...". Indeed, in 2005, a federal judge in the United States ruled that the religious beliefs known as intelligent design cannot be taught in science classes as an alternative to Darwin's theory.

The meme of Creation gave birth to the Sabbath meme. The motivation was the desire to imitate God's rest on Day Seven. From generation to generation, the Jews celebrate Sabbath as a day of enlightenment and spirituality free of a daily work. It also became an additional meaningful sign of the Covenant and commemoration of the Exodus.

Arno Penzias, previously mentioned as a key contributor to the Big Bang model, was born into a Jewish family in 1933 in Munich, Bavaria, the very heart of the Nazi movement. Hitler became Chancellor that very year. This was undoubtedly a case of being at the worst place at the worst time. On top of that, his father was a Polish citizen, which immediately doubled the crime of the young couple. At the last moment in 1939, the family made a narrow escape, fleeing to Britain and then to New York. Arno's father got a job as janitor, his mother as a garment worker. Even impoverished families could get education for their children, which was the true greatness of the United States. Arno earned his Ph.D. in radio astronomy from the prestigious Columbia University Department of Physics. In 1978, Penzias, preparing himself for the award ceremony of the Nobel Prize in physics that he had won together with Wilson, was concerned about the obligatory tuxedo. Later, he recalled: "I wanted, if I can call it that, a Jewish tuxedo, something made in the garment district. My mother worked there, and a whole generation of Jewish immigrants put the next generation through college by working there....I wanted the tuxedo to be me and not some sort of costume".

Meme and the City

The vast majority of Diaspora Jews were city dwellers: discriminatory regulations and ghettos forced them to adapt to urban environment, which had left its mark on the Jewish mentality and had been the main reason for the famous Jewish communication skills. It seems, however, that a tendency for a communal lifestyle can be tracked back to ancient Israelites as the Qumran scrolls could confirm.

In the Jewish national memory, small impoverished towns of a western part of the Imperial Russia and Poland, the shtetels, are associated with Hasidic scholars; later this role was taken over by Brookline, USA. Odessa, a Russian port on the Black Sea, had a long history of Jewish presence which faded with mass emigration to Israel and the United States in the second half of the twentieth century; this city was well-known for its Jewish wunderkinds, gangs, and criminal jargon. Isaac Babel, who was born in Odessa and lived there during the turbulent years of pogroms and revolutions, perpetuated some of these memes in his brilliant novels. In his own style, Woody Allen seems to do the same for Jewish New Yorkers.

With return to the Promised Land, Jews, finally free of the hindering influence of their host, were expected to create a unique urban culture of their own; their lauded creativity and imagination should come into play, at last. Nothing of the sort happened. Tel Aviv is merely a large urban center of commerce, finances, traffic, and entertainment and does not bear any special trademark, similarly to other modern Israeli cities.

There are two ancient settlements, Hebron and Jerusalem, inherited from the Hebrews and subjected to the ferocity of a long and tangled history, which ignite imagination, passion, and controversy. The Jewish singularity has begun in Hebron, when Abraham bought the *Cave of Machpelah* and declared himself as "a stranger and sojourner with you".

With the exception of periods of anti-Jewish violence, there always was a Jewish presence in Hebron. Paul Johnson described the meme of Hebron in a way which cannot be surpassed: "…Hebron reflects the long, tragic history of the Jews and their unrivalled capacity to survive their misfortunes. David was anointed king there, first of Judah, and then of all Israel…. From 1266 the Jews were forbidden to enter the cave to pray. They were permitted only to ascend seven steps by the side of the eastern wall. On the fourth step they inserted their petition to God in a hole bored six feet six inches through the stone. Sticks were used to push the bits of paper through until they fell into the Cave…. So when the historian visits Hebron today, he asks himself: where are all those peoples which once held the lace? Where are the Canaanites? Where are the Edomites? Where are the ancient Hellenes and the Romans, the Byzantines, the Franks, the Mamluks and the Ottomans? They have vanished into time, irrevocably. But the Jews are still in Hebron".

Moreover, historians believe that several militant Arab clans in the area, the fierce followers of Islam, are in fact of Jewish origins; they converted hundreds years ago. A genetic similarity between Arabs and Jews is no accident.

Much more can be said about Jerusalem, which was literally shaped by memes; it is an explosive tangle of contradictions, beliefs, and passions, perhaps the mixture of the most intense Jewish memes. In the best of Jewish traditions, even its very name is confusing: when translated from Hebrew, it may mean "Heritage of Peace" or "City of Peace", yet for the last two millennia there was nothing more removed from this city than peace. Jerusalem's history is full of wars, violence, and controversies, the strength of which parallels only the beauty of its hilly landscape, the intensity of its streaming sun-light, and the vastness of its spiritual associations. The city is vital for the three monotheistic religions.

David captured the city from Jebusites and, appreciating its strategic location, expanded it and made the capital of the Kingdom of Israel. Jerusalem was the capital of the Kingdom of Judah for almost four hundred years. The city had been considered to be a religious shrine since the ninth century B.C.E; it was the home for both of the Temples. It endured the devastating wars with the Assyrians, Babylonians, and Romans and only in 6 C.E. lost its independence and came under direct Roman control. After the Great Jewish Revolt, Titus ravaged it again in 70 C.E; only a part of the external wall of the Second Temple, known as the Western Wall or the Wailing Wall, endured. In the second century the Romans began to remodel Jerusalem as a pagan center, provoking another revolt led by Bar Kochba. According to estimates, the Romans killed more that half-a-million Israelites, and then renamed the city *Aelia Capitolina*, to stress its new pagan essence. With a typical Roman "generosity of soul", they did permit Jews to enter Jerusalem annually on *Tisha B'Av* but only to mourn over their destroyed Temple. With the rise of Christianity, the city became a focus of Christian activity, including anti-Jewish violence. In 335–6 C.E., the Church of the Holy Sepulcher was erected at the site of Jesus' crucifixion. No less than five different Christian communities presently have rights there.

The time had come for the Muslim domination which, in general, was more tolerant. Umar ibn al-Khattab, a Caliph, captured the city in 638 C.E. and granted the Jews the rights to live and worship in Jerusalem, thus lifting four hundred years ban. The two mosques, the Dome of the Rock and Al-Aqsa, were built close to the ruins of the Jewish Temple. In the first Crusade of 1099, the city was again occupied and the Muslim and Jewish populations massacred. Saladin recaptured Jerusalem and allowed free worship of all religions. Then there was a long succession of occupiers: Germans, Arabs, Christians, Tatars, Egyptians, Mamelukes, and Turks. One gets the impression that there was a waiting list of tribes and nations standing in line to take over the city and alter its destiny. The rule of Suleiman the Magnificent and subsequent Ottoman sultans was a period of relative peace and religious freedom.

A priest, Felix Fabri, who visited Jerusalem in 1482, described it with the medieval Christian intolerance as "a dwelling place of diverse nations of the world, and is, as it were, a collection of all manner of abominations". Who were those abominations? The list was endless: Saracens, Greeks, Syrians, Jacobites, Abyssianians, Nestorians, Armenians, Gregorians, Maronites, Turcomans, Bedouins, Mamelukes, and, of course, as Fabri did not fail to mention, "the most accursed of all", Jews.

For hundreds of years, Jerusalem was a small city with mixed population of roughly eight thousand; it was largely a jumble of ethnic neighborhoods. Religious tensions run high even within communities of the same affiliation: a neutral Muslim kept the keys to the Church of the Holy Sepulcher to soften the rivalry among the Catholic, Greek Orthodox, Armenian, Ethiopian, and Coptic churches. There was a change in the ethnic makeup of the city in the nineteenth century, when Jews became the largest group as a result of immigrations from Eastern Europe and Arab countries. They once again displayed a pioneer spirit and were the first to build a settlement outside the walls, the New City. The Russian Orthodox Church built its own compound near the Old City.

A new era began with the British victory over the Turks in 1917. To display his delight, General Edmund Allenby demonstratively entered the Holy City on foot. This was the beginning of the British Mandate; the British tried to improve the management of the city and to standardize construction. In the thirties, the Hadassah Medical Center and Hebrew University were instituted as integral part of the Jewish community. Riots and violence also marked the British rule, including pogroms in 1920 and the bombing of the King David Hotel in 1946, all in the midst of increasing Jewish immigration. The partition plan, approved by the United Nations in 1947, failed to materialize and the British Mandate ended in May 1948. As a result of the War of Independence, Israel gained control over the western part of the New City, outside the wall, while the eastern part, along with the Old City, was annexed by Jordan.

This left the Jews without access to their holiest sites. However, following the Six-Day War in 1967, Israel gained control over Jerusalem in its entirety. The ancient Moroccan Quarter adjacent to the Western Wall was demolished to make space for a large plaza intended to accommodate Jewish worshippers. Presently, Jews, Christians, and Muslims have free access to their holy sites, except for temporary limitations due to security concerns, which remain a major issue in Jerusalem. The Al-Aqsa Mosque, built on the site of the Temple Mount, is an especially sensitive spot. Religious restrictions allow Jews to visit the Mount in small groups, but they are supposed to take special care not to trespass on the possible site of the Holy of Holies.

Given this unique history, it is only natural that the international status of Jerusalem is highly controversial. Presently, both Israel and Palestine see it as their capital and have enacted the appropriate legislation. The United Nations resolution 478 declared that the Israeli law of 1988, which treated Jerusalem as Israel's capital, was null and void; still, this document was adopted without the vital American support. Moreover, in 1995 the Congress passed a special Act requesting relocation of the United States Embassy to Jerusalem as Israel's capital "no later than May 31, 1999". This was not the end of the story, as the U.S. President would systematically suspend the move. Recently, both Congress and President have restated their polar positions. Israelis may take comfort in the fact that the Congressional resolution prevails from a legal point of view. Only Costa Rica and El Salvador keep their embassies in Jerusalem. The Holy See prefers internationalization of the city; the United Kingdom "regards the status of Jerusalem as still to be determined in permanent status negotiations between the parties…". The British elaborate further: "Pending agreement, we recognize de facto Israeli control of West Jerusalem but consider East Jerusalem to be occupied territory. We recognize no sovereignty over the city."

President Bill Clinton authored an imaginative suggestion for resolving the problem of sovereignty over the Temple Mount: the top with the mosques belongs to the Muslims, the bottom with various archeological findings to the Jews. The late King Hussein of Jordan went as far as to propose the transfer of all the rights over the Temple Mount to God, its real owner; just declare that sovereignty belongs to the Creator and you have almost solved the problem of the Holy Sites in Jerusalem.

How was it possible to create and maintain such a dangerous and absolute mess of memes over such a long a period of time? The answer lies in religious beliefs. For Jews, this city is the pinnacle of their faith. When they speak of the Promised Land they are referring mainly to Jerusalem, at least from a spiritual point of view. In 1948, the national poet, Uri Zvi

Greenberg, wrote that "Israel without the mountain would not be Israel". For the two millennia of the Diaspora, they kept saying to themselves with Jewish persistence (some would say, stubbornness): "Next Year in Jerusalem" and "if I forget thee, O Jerusalem, let my right hand fall asunder.".

The holiness of Jerusalem was embedded in the Torah, psalms, prayers, festivals, and mourning. Recently, the Maltz Museum of the Jewish community was inaugurated in far away Cleveland, Ohio, USA. It was built of Jerusalem limestone quarried in Israel. Synagogues all over the world should be oriented so that the prayers face Jerusalem; in Jerusalem a praying man or woman must face the Western Wall and, if at the Western Wall, he must face the site of the Holy of Holies, which is believed to be presently under Dome of the Rock. It is the oldest Jerusalem synagogue built in 1267 that illustrates best the full intensity of Jewish feelings: when Ramban left Spain and immigrated to the Promised Land, he was able to locate only ten surviving Jews in the city, devastated by Crusaders. Together they built the synagogue, which is still there.

Though the extreme Jewish adherence to Jerusalem seems to have no parallel, Christians and Muslims have developed their own memes. The Christian version is a superstructure over Jewish beliefs. Jesus grew up as a child in Jerusalem. Jesus healed and preached there, including at the Temple. His Last Supper took place in Jerusalem as well as his suffering on the way to Golgotha, his crucifixion, and resurrection. The Church of the Holy Sepulchre seems to be the holiest place for Christians.

Jerusalem is also one of the pilgrimage cities for Islam, though not as valuable as Mecca. By a Muslim meme, Mohammed ascended to heaven from Jerusalem. The two mosques, Dome of the Rock and Al-Aqsa, were erected there with the former containing one of the oldest stone inscriptions of verses from the Koran.

Historic events, inspired by memes, in turn affect and could alter the latter. Prior to the Six-Day War, Israel was almost a Third World country, and Jews had no access to the remnants of their Temple. The Arab and Iranian sources had no difficulties to acknowledge the fact that the Al-Aqsa mosque was built on the site of the destroyed Jewish Temple. Since 1967, with Jews in control of Jerusalem and Israel emerging as a developed country, Muslim scholars suddenly discovered that "the legend about the Jewish temple is the greatest historic crime of forgery", that the Western Wall is a holy Muslim site, and that the Al-Aqsa Mosque was built by Adam, thus predating Jesus as well as Moses. Late Arafat, President of the Palestinian Authority, was said to stick to these claims in his last failed negotiations with the Israelis.

Geopolitical ambitions and economic interests caused both the First and Second World Wars. Because of their intensity, the memes of Jerusalem, those related to the Temple Mount in particular, which influence roughly two billion Christians, two billion Muslims, and thirteen million Jews, may develop a lethal strain and trigger the Third World War, which could well be the last one.

In 1969, Michael Rohan, a tourist from Australia, in an outburst of providential inspiration, set fire to the Al-Aqsa Mosque, which resulted in the mass rioting of Muslims. This was a case of the *Jerusalem Syndrome*, a group of mental illnesses precipitated by a visit to the Holy City and described in the thirties by psychiatrist Heinz Herman: a person without a recorded psychiatric history turns psychotic as a result of the visit and associated religious delusions. Another account of the syndrome was given much earlier by Fabri, mentioned in the above. Psychiatrists think that Jerusalem maniacs, mostly Jewish or Christian pilgrims, come to the Holy City ready to go crazy, and were in fact mentally ill prior to the visit. Usually it is schizophrenia or manic depression. The visit only worsens their conditions. A person thinking of himself as the Messiah would come to the city to formalize his status; a founder of new religion or a sect is another typical case. In average, about ten patients a year are treated. There is no evidence that the syndrome had ever affected a Muslim, but we may speculate that the pilgrimage to Mecca would precipitate a similar phenomenon.

What's in a Name?

Jews were among the first to ascribe a special meaning to a name. Indeed, the Jewish God attached major importance to a name. In Genesis, God promised Abraham that a great nation would result from his seed and would possess the land of Canaan; then God went on as follows: "Neither shall your name any more be called Abram, but your name shall be Abraham; for the father of a multitude of nations have I made thee. And I will make you exceeding fruitful, and I will make nations of you, and kings shall come out of you." By changing your name you may affect your fate. The Talmud notes that "Four things can abrogate the decree of man and they are: charity, supplication, change of name and change of action." Moreover, the name follows a person into his afterlife.

The Jewish God has several names, the first and most significant of them is *YHWH*, which is known as the *Tetragrammaton*. It appears in the Torah 6,823 times. Jews have believed for many centuries that the very pronunciation of God's name is sinful. Since Hebrew makes use of consonants only, the exact way this name is spoken remains uncertain, but most agree that this should be something like *Yahweh*. There are speculations that this word is somehow connected with the verb "to be" (in Hebrew). Because of the commandment defining restrictions put on the use of YHWH, there is another word, *Adonai*, which translates to English as Lord. In conversation, many Jews refer to God as *HaShem*, which is the Hebrew translation for "the Name". Still, other Biblical words are *Elohim* or *Elion* or *El*. The latter gives rise to such names as Daniel, which is translated as "God is my Judge", or Gabriel, translated as "Hero of God". Other names of God bring to light his versatility: *Baruch Hu* (Blessed be He), *Elohei Avraham, Elohei Yitzchak ve Elohei Yaacov* (God of Abraham, God of Isaac, God of Jacob), *Avinu Malkeinu* (Our Father Our King), *Melech ha-Melachim* (The King of Kings). The Kabbalah, the Jewish esoteric teachings, may go as far as to claim that the entire Torah, each letter, word or punctuation mark, which all conceal divine meaning, is, in fact, one long name of God merely broken up into phrases and words to facilitate man's understanding. In order to stress the holiness of God's name, there are elaborate rules to be complied with while writing it. In particular, one must prepare oneself mentally; once one starts writing he should not stop or interrupt until it is finished. If an error is made, a circle must be drawn around it to indicate nullification and the page must be destroyed.

Sephardim have adopted Spanish names since the Middle Ages, however, in Europe, Ashkenazim still adhered to the old tradition of using a personal name plus the paternal name. The Austrian law of 1787 forced Jews to adopt German-sounding names. The move was intended to facilitate taxation and conscription of the Jewish population and was one of the fines Jews paid for their emancipation. Names like Schwartz (black), Weiss (white), Gross (big) and Klein (small) became widespread. One had to bribe a governmental official in order to get a "better" name like Rosenfeld, Diamant or Berg. Russian Jews began to adopt Russian names as a part of their assimilation; these were often Christianized Hebrew names, like Misha, Yuri, or Semyon. American Jews preferred Anglo-Saxon names, like Morton or Malcolm; this, in fact, was a simple substitute for conversion. Times had changed. In order to have a public career one could merely adopt a Christian name, which often worked. If Disraeli would have lived in the twentieth century, he might possibly have chosen this way instead of conversion. I recall myself as a child watching the movie "*Spartacus*" with much admiration. Kirk Douglas played the main role; this Hollywood mega-star of Belarusian Jewish parents was born as Isser Demsky.

Since the beginning of the twentieth century, with the influx of Jews to pre-statehood Palestine and then to Israel, there was a massive trend of changing names to reflect a new identity: Eizen became Barzelay, Rose became Shoshana and Boris became Baruch. The names of Lior, Tal, and Sapir, could be given to boys as well as girls; Noa for a girl and Uri for a boy are presently the most popular names in Israel. Religious Jews, in particular those residing in settlements, prefer traditional names, Moshe, Esther, David. Some would stress religious affiliation, like Emuna (Faith) or Tohar (Purity).

In order to stress the importance of a person's name, Israeli rabbis recently published a list of those, which are not recommended for children; among them, Ariel and Omri: the former may anger the angel Ariel, the latter was the name of a Biblical king of bad deeds. Names that include the suffix or prefix "el" meaning God in Hebrew, should also be avoided.

The Interior Ministry banned the names "God", "Hitler", and "Bin Laden", from being registered in its population records.

God's name is itself a meme and, as such, it evolves. In Islam there are ninety nine names of God, all of them listed in the Koran. Allah is the first name with the rest mainly referring to God's attributes. The hundredth name is a mystery and is, by some interpretations, the real name of God. Sufism, one of the Islamic sects, attaches much importance to the hundredth name of God and sees a deep religious meaning in it. Many first names around the world are, in fact, derivatives of Jewish names, such as Eva, Maria, John, Ivan, Sara, Illya, Semyon, Musa, Suleiman, and Daud.

The association of person's name with his or her character and destiny are fundamental to numerology; still, the very idea was borrowed from the Bible. Numerology, which is so popular today, suggests that your name is an expression of your essence. As various occult theories ascribe magic power to human names, this matter may not be as innocent as it seems. The Soviet cosmic effort in the sixties unexpectedly provided an illustration. Rumors had it that German Titov was initially selected to be recorded in history as the first human to visit outer space with Yuri Gagarin as his substitute. Titov was considered the more brilliant of the two. The communist boss, Nikita Khrushchev, overturned that decision on the grounds that Titov's first name, German, was not of Russian origin. The first cosmonaut had to be a Russian and bear a genuine Russian name as nothing should spoil a propaganda festival to be held after the first cosmic voyage. Therefore, Gagarin was the first cosmonaut to blast off from the Baikonur cosmodrom. Devastated Titov never fully recovered; perhaps Khrushchev, who harbored anti-Semitic feelings, would also have been devastated, if he had known that the name "Yuri" may have been derived from the Jewish name Uri (Uriel). Moreover, a few years later, Gagarin was tragically killed in a plane crash.

Black, White, Kosher

The Jewish God has kept a watchful eye over the Jewish deeds and thoughts and retaliated with heavy punishments for a breach of the Covenant. These often took place on the two specific days, *Shivah Asar B'Tammuz* and *Tisha B'Av*. On Shivah Asar B'Tammuz, Moshe descended Mount Sinai and broke the Tablets of the Covenant, when he found his tribe, the potential Chosen People, worshipping a golden calf; Romans broke through the walls of Jerusalem and later placed an idol in the courtyard of the Second Temple. More recent tragic events include: destruction of the Jewish Quarter in Prague in 1559, liquidation of Kovno's ghetto in 1944, and deadly bombing of the Jewish community center in Buenos Aires, Argentina, in 1994. That is why, the seventeenth day of the Jewish month of Tammuz, which overlaps June and July, marks the beginning of the three week period of mourning. It reaches its climax on the ninth of the Jewish month of Av and often coincides with the ninth of August, Tisha B'Av in Hebrew.

Still, the most tragic events took place on Tisha B'Av, which starts at sundown on the eighth day of the Jewish month of Av and terminates at sundown on the ninth day of the same month. On this day, both of the Temples were demolished, the first by the Babylonians in 586 B.C.E., and the second by the Romans in 70 C.E.; the fortress of Betar, the last one to hold out against the Romans during Bar Kochba's uprising, was destroyed; in 1095, Pope Urban II declared a Crusade, which led to bloody Jewish pogroms; in 1492, the Spanish monarchs, Queen Isabella and King Ferdinand, picked Tisha B'Av as the last chance for Jews to safely leave Spain; War World I broke out, triggering the chain of events, which led to the rise of the Nazis, World War II, and the Holocaust.

These tragic events cover the period of nearly three millennia; yet Jews take care to keep all the records and passionately pray in their remembrance. Remarkably, Judaism speculates that the Messiah will be born on Tisha B'Av to save the world. Though factions of religious Zionism tried to abolish commemoration of Tisha B'Av and thereby honor the re-creation of Israel, this meme survives in its strict original form.

But there are also festivals. The Passover, *Pesach* in Hebrew, is one of them. It begins on sundown of the fourteenth day of the Jewish month of Nissan and lasts for a week; Diaspora Jews usually observe it for eight days. The word "Pesach" means to pass through, pass over, or spare; in the present context it refers to the Biblical description of the firstborn plague, when God "passed over" and thus spared the Jewish houses. It is a Holy Day which commemorates the Exodus of the Israelites from Egypt, a key event of Jewish history. There are three main rules for the Jews to fulfill during the holidays: eating *matzoh,* or unleavened bread, avoiding any food containing leavening and retelling the story of the Exodus from Egypt. Why unleavened bread? In their haste from Egypt, the Jews had neither time nor conditions to properly prepare bread.

Passover is a happy family holiday and often celebrated even by non-observant Jews. The first and seventh days are full holidays, as are also the second and eighth days for Diaspora Jews. A special dinner, *Seder,* is arranged as a family or communal gathering. This includes a ceremony of serving special meals and reading the prayer book, the *Passover Haggadah,* which is the story of the Exodus. It is believed that more than eighty percent of Jews attend a Pesach Seder each year.

A mutant version of the meme of Passover was adopted by Christians. If for the Jews, Passover symbolizes deliverance from Egyptian bondage, for Christians it represents liberation from the serfdom of sin. On this occasion, the crucifixion of Jesus is recalled as a sacrifice of Passover Lamb, intended to deliver mankind from the Kingdom of Sin. Details of the observance may vary from one Christian group to another.

In addition to Passover, there are two other major festivities: *Shavu'ot* and *Sukkot.* Jews count forty nine days from the second day of Passover to the day before Shavu'ot, or seven full weeks; seven is *sheva* in Hebrew, from which the name originates. It is also known as the Festival of the First Fruits, as it signals the beginning of a harvest season. It is also the Festival of the Giving of the Torah, which complements deliverance from Egyptian bondage, marked by Passover. Work is not permitted during Shavu'ot.

The festival of Sukkot begins on the fifth day after Yom Kippur and lasts for seven days; it also has a dual meaning, marking both the forty-year period of Jews wandering in the Sinai desert following the Exodus from Egypt and the joy of the harvest. Sukkot means "booths" and refers to temporary shelters or huts erected to symbolize the Jewish people wandering in the wilderness. No work is permitted on the first two days of the celebrations. Another tradition of Sukkot involves the so-called Four Species: a citron (*etrog* in Hebrew), a palm branch (*lulav*), two willow branches (*aravot*), and three myrtle branches (*hassadim*). There are two interpretations of the significance of the Four Species. According to the first interpretation, they symbolize various parts of the human body. The palm branch represents the spine, the myrtle leaf represents the eye, the willow leaf represents the mouth, and the citron symbolizes the heart. The second interpretation deals with various "types" of Jews. The citron, because of its good taste and scent, exemplifies Jews who excel in both, knowledge of the Torah and good deeds. The palm branch, which has no scent but delivers tasty fruit, exemplifies Jews who are knowledgeable in the Torah but do not carry out good deeds. The myrtle leaf, which is tasteless but has a strong scent, symbolizes Jews who have done good deeds but have little knowledge. Finally, the willow, which is tasteless and scentless, symbolizes Jews without either. Keeping the Four Species together stresses the value of Jewish unity.

A young beauty, Esther, and her cousin, Mordecai, are heroes of the story of *Purim* told in the Book of Esther. Ahasuerus, King of Persia, fell in love with Esther and made her his queen, presumably without knowing she was Jewish. The villain, Haman, counselor to the king, plotted to exterminate the Jewish people. He told the king: "There is a certain people scattered abroad and dispersed among the peoples in all the provinces of your realm. Their laws are different from those of every other people, and they do not observe the king's laws; therefore it is not befitting to the king to tolerate them." Ahasuerus decided to leave the Jews at Haman's mercy and the latter was ready to destroy all of them. Persuaded by Mordecai, Esther, risking her life, told the king of Haman's plot; the Jews were saved and Haman hanged on the gallows that had been prepared for Mordecai. Purim is celebrated on the fourteenth day of Adar, which is usually in March and is one of the most joyful holidays on the Jewish calendar It is customary to stamp feet, boo, hiss, and rattle whenever the name of Haman is mentioned. Jews are also commanded to eat, drink and be merry; the Talmud elaborates that a Jew should drink until he cannot tell the difference between "cursed be Haman" and "blessed be Mordecai". Jews hold carnivals, and send out gifts of food or drink and make gifts to charity. Men, women, and children enjoy dressing up in costumes and masks and parading. In memory of the story, Iranian Jews are sometimes referred to as "Esthers's Children"; Esther, a Persian queen, is presumably buried in the city of Hamadan, in Western Iran.

Besides the above annual events, Judaism took care to sharpen up the Jewish identity on a daily, if not hourly, basis. Circumcision is a permanent handy sign a Jew bears almost from birth to death. The same is *kashrut*. Basic restrictions of the Jewish diet are set down in the Book of Leviticus with further details put down in the Oral Law. The Hebrew word *kosher*, which signifies compliance with the rules of kashrut, was integrated into the English language, meaning "proper" or "approved".

There are various reasons behind the Jewish observance of kashrut. Indeed, centuries ago, Maimonides stressed that the laws given by God always have a good rationale. The obvious one was a healthy hygiene: birds of prey may get disease from the carrion, which they consume, and shellfish, being a sort of filter, may absorb toxins or parasites. Pork, if undercooked, may harbor parasites; moreover, as we presently know, pigs are among the main incubators for a variety of flu viruses. Kashrut requires checking the lungs of animals for possible adhesions, which may indicate the presence of tuberculosis. In general, there is a total ban on slaughtering deseased animals for food. Kashrut involves elaborate regulations concerning kosher slaughtering and procedures of proper certification. Animals with cloven hooves and sea creatures without fins or scales are forbidden in the diet. It is still a mystery why the Israelites were forbidden from mixing milk and meat products, though I would not exclude a possibility of scientific explanation in the future. Many Jews comply with some rules of kashrut and violate the others. Like circumcision, kashrut is also a declaration of the membership in a particular tribe, keeping its own rules given by God. Its observance is also a daily drill of self-control and discipline.

Shabut in Arabic, *Barbus grybus* in the scientific Latin, is a kosher fish living in the rivers of Iraq, Syria, and Iran; it may reach a length of two meters and a weight of sixty kilograms. For a Jewish gourmet, this fish is a delight, as its taste is similar to pork. This is noted in the Babylonian Talmud. (How, exactly, experts of those times, presumably the strict keepers of kashrut who never touched pork, had reached this conclusion remains a mystery.) That is why, one such Shabut was recently brought to Israel from Iran in a clandestine operation; Israeli experts are studying the possibility of breeding of the "pork of the sea".

Esoterica and Folklore

Observing dietary laws, circumcision, festivities, and memorials to enhance their identity as an ethnic group, the Jews did not give up what was perhaps their most powerful weapon: imagination. The Torah already contained quite a few mystical events, among them: the binding of Isaac, Jacob's ladder to heaven, and Moses' burning bush. The teaching of Kabbalah, which in Hebrew means Receiving, takes the Jewish mysticism to its extremity. The Kabbalah claims an extremely high status for itself: it is the mystical, concealed, inner meaning of the Torah and part of the Oral Law. Every word of the holy Torah, every Hebrew letter or number contains supernatural meanings and secrets, which can be discovered by studies of the Kabbalah, which became an integral part of the Jewish phenomenon.

The story of Jacob's ladder is as follows: "...And he dreamed that there was a ladder set up on the earth, and the top of it reached to heaven; and behold, the angels of God were ascending and descending on it! And behold, the LORD stood above it and said, "I am the LORD, the God of Abraham your father and the God of Isaac; the land on which you lie I will give to you and to your descendants; and your descendants shall be like the dust of the earth, and you shall spread abroad to the west and to the east and to the north and to the south; and by you and your descendants shall all the families of the earth bless themselves. Behold, I am with you and will keep you wherever you go, and will bring you back to this land; for I will not leave you until I have done that of which I have spoken to you."

The power of imagination behind this description is outstanding; still the Kabbalah goes much further and manipulates the Light, Angels, spirits, symbols, incarnations and transmigrations, positive and negative energies. Imagination in general seems to be inherent in Judaism. When somebody dies, instead of merely saying "he (or she) is dead", Jews may say: "he (or she) went to his (or her) world". The Kabbalah makes no definite distinction between physical and spiritual realms; the blood is the soul; objective and subjective are closely interrelated. God created both matter and spirit, but God is neither. This systematic resort to strong mental images was perhaps borrowed from exact sciences which also resort to imagination. The German physicist Max Plank wrote in his autobiography: "When the pioneer in science sends forth the groping fingers of his thoughts, he must have a vivid, intuitive imagination, for new ideas are not generated by deduction, but by artistically creative imagination"; Einstein bluntly commented that "imagination is more important than knowledge".

Sefer Yetzirah, which means "Book of Creation", is the mystical text, which appeared in the medieval era. It was attributed to Abraham and in its entirety assumed to be accessible only to select groups of Jewish scholars. According to a Talmudic story, its power was so extraordinary that two medieval rabbis, experts in the Sefer Yetzirah, were said to habitually "create" a calf each Friday and eat it as their Sabbath dinner. This text was also used, as legends have it, to fabricate semi-robotic creatures, known as *golems,* out of clay or mud. Other mystics believed that a golem could be produced with the help of the Divine Name, each syllable being in charge of a particular limb or organ of the golem.

The Kabbalah began to flourish as a branch of the Oral Law alongside the Talmud with the appearance of its central masterpiece, the book of *Zohar* (splendor); most experts agree that it was written either by Rabbi Shimon Bar Yohai between the first and third centuries C.E. or by Rabbi Moses de Leon in the thirteenth century. There are two arguments in favor of the first version: from one generation to the next, our understanding of the Torah gets vaguer because the Divine event on Mount Sinai becomes further removed from us and the probability of re-creating such an extraordinary text diminishes with time; second, hiding from the Romans, Rabbi Shimon spent thirteen years in a cave near the town of Pequin in Galilee, which should have given him the necessary inspiration.

Still, the authorship of the Zohar remains a subject of controversy. Kabalists even suggest that the teaching was presented in its oral form to Moses on Mount Sinai together with the Ten Commandments and then revealed to Rabbi Shimon by the prophet Elijah. In a sense, Rabbi Shimon was a reincarnation of Moses. Even today, tens of thousands visit his burial site annually at Meron near Safed on *Lag B'Omer*, the day of Rabbi Shimon's death.

One of the key figures among the Jewish medieval mystics was Moses Nachmanides born in Spain in 1194. Being a physician, like Maimonides (Rambam), he was an antithesis of the latter in religious matters, focusing on hidden meanings of the Jewish scriptures. Nachmanides contributed much to Kabalistic views on the creation of the universe, promoting ideas about the unity of time and matter, which, in a paradoxical way, were similar to concepts of modern physics. He dared to participate in public religious debates, aggressively refuting Christian dogmas; a famous encounter of this sort took place before King Jaime I of Spain in 1263. Nachmanides was expelled from Spain for his assertive defense of Judaism and moved to Palestine where he died in 1270.

After the expulsion from Spain in 1492, Jewish mystics came to Palestine and finally found themselves settled in the mountain town of Safed in the Upper Galilee, thereby starting the Golden Age of Kabbalah; several schools of Jewish mysticism blossomed in Safed for a century. It was once again a manifestation of the incredible Jewish persistence: instead of converting and remaining in Spain, they fled as far as the Galilee and submerged themselves into the obscure but rewarding world of esoterica. So, in a paradoxical way, the Kabbalah owes much to the Spanish monarchs, Isabella and Ferdinand, the authors of the expulsion order.

Many of the great kabalists of that time were Sephardic. Rabbi Moses Cordovero wrote the first elaborated commentary on the Zohar; Rabbi Isaac Lurie, known as *Ari Hakodosh*, which means Holy Lion in Hebrew, developed his own method of appreciating secrets of the Zohar, the Lurianic system. He was born in Jerusalem in 1534 and later taken to Egypt by his mother, where he spent his youth. In 1569, he also settled in Safed. A controversial medieval occultist Nostradamus was a French Jew by birth, but his family converted and practiced Catholicism. He studied Kabbalah, astrology, and medicine. His followers credit him for prophesizing the French Revolution, the atomic bomb, the rise and fall of the Nazis, the rise and fall of Communism, among many other crucial historic events. Skeptics point out the ambiguous character of his prophesies which can be given to a variety of interpretations, and sarcastically comment that he was "always accurate at predicting events *after* they happen". Nostradamus was lucky to have been overlooked by the Inquisition.

A modern stage of the Kabbalah began in the twentieth century, when Rabbi Yehuda Ashlag translated the entire Zohar from Aramaic into Hebrew. The spread of Hasidic Judaism, with its mystic overtones, as well as the influence of religious Zionism, which sees the recreation of Israel as the beginning of salvation, were also sources of inspiration for modern kabalists.

Following the Torah, the Kabbalah considers God as perfect, almighty, and complete; He lacks absolutely nothing. But there is also a modification: the Kabbalah states explicitly that God is good, He is the source of all that is positive; God desires to share, impart His goodness, which is the *Desire to Impart*. We may percept this goodness as the Light charged with positive energy. God's energy is infinite, that is why his energy does not diminish. There is the notion of *En-Sof*, infinity in Hebrew, which reflects the idea of the original perfect infinite world, the world of harmony, and the notion of *Sefirot*, "vessels" or "agencies" designed to emanate God's Light on man. Sefirot were God's tools for creating the world. There are ten of them: *Keter* (Crown), *Hochma* (Wisdom), *Bina* (Intelligence), *Hesed* (Mercy), *Gevurah* or *Din* (Judgment), *Tiferet* (Beauty), *Netzah* (Victory), *Hod* (Glory), *Yesod* (Foundation), and *Malkhut* (Kingdom).

In direct contrast to the Desire to Impart, there is a mundane word with its *Desire to Receive*; the world is actually made of the Desire to Receive. Human selfishness and materialism are manifestations of the Desire to Receive. There is interplay between the Desire to Impart and Desire to Receive. An individual may compensate his Desire to Receive by drawing positive energy, the Light, into himself; but there must be a balance between the two. The book of Zohar comments that "The natural consequence of eating unearned bread, of receiving something that is not earned by labor and endeavor is embarrassment and shame! He eats the Bread of Shame". The special notion of *Tsimsum*, restriction, exists to express the need for controlling the Desire to Receive. Thus, giving and taking is one of the central issues of the Kabbalah. Another favorite subject is *gilgul neshamot*, which is almost synonymous with reincarnation; the word *gilgul* means "cycles" or "rotation", while *neshamot* means "souls". Its complicated rules, written by Rabbi Isaac Lurie, are described in *Shaar ha Gilgulim*, which is "Gate of Reincarnations" in Hebrew.

Kabalists like to employ graphical illustrations for their abstract notions. For example, there are interrelationships among Sefirot and parts of a human body. In particular, Crown corresponds, as could be expected, to head, Mercy to the right arm, Beauty to breast, etc. Foundation is associated with genitals, which is instructive.

The themes of *Sitrei Torah* are the most deeply hidden teachings of the Kabbalah; one must be over forty, male and married to approach these subjects; the Zohar contains sections, which are specifically marked as containing Sitrei Torah. The basic teachings are known as *Ta'amei Torah* and are suitable for everyone.

In general, the book of Zohar often develops its own interpretation of the stories of the Torah. The binding of Isaac is a typical example: God tested Isaac to the same extent to that he tested Abraham. The Kabbalah stresses the total submission of Isaac to the will of God and discusses it in the context of a balance between Gevurah, or Din (Judgment) and Hesed (Mercy). Islam developed its own version of this meme, suggesting that Ishmael was to be sacrificed, not Isaac.

The book of Zohar also contains a remarkable interpretation of a crucial issue of the Chosen People, explicitly stated by God when he met Moses on Mount Sinai; the wording is so strong and melodious that it merits repetition: "Ye have seen what I did to the Egyptians, and how I bare you on eagles' wings and brought you unto myself. Now therefore, if ye will obey my voice in deed, and keep my covenant, then ye shall be a peculiar treasure unto me above all people". The Zohar claims that the Torah was first offered to other nations who rejected it: "the children of

Esau and...the children of Ishmael...would not accept it". The offer, according to the Zohar's version, was made via angels Samael and Rahab, responsible, respectively, for Esau and Ishmael. The Ten Commandments were the obstacle: Samael did not like the premise of "Thou shalt not kill", as "if there are no wars, my power will pass away from the world"; Rahab rejected it because of prohibition of adultery, and referred to the blessing given to Adam: "Be fruitful and multiply". Kabalists suggest that "God...knew that if he gave the Torah to Israel without telling (the other nations), they would every day pursue them and kill them for it". It seems it did not help anyway. If this interpretation of the Zohar is true, there was nothing genetic about the Covenant from the very beginning, which is in accordance with the traditional Jewish beliefs noted earlier.

In their search for concealed meanings, kabalists also turn to numbers. Because in Hebrew there is a correspondence between a letter and a number, say, Aleph stands for 1 and Bet for 2, and so on, you may think of a numerical representation of a word or phrase and manipulate the numbers. Furthermore, as every letter of the Jewish Scriptures, first of all the Torah, was literally given by God, you may discover their hidden meanings by studying numerical patterns emerging from these scriptures. The basic assumption is that words of the same numerical values have similar "quality". This is precisely what the *Gematria*, a kind of numerology, deals with. The Zohar goes further in trying to establish a correspondence between the twenty two letters of the Hebrew alphabet and the ten Sefirot. Appendix B contains a basic chart for converting the Hebrew letters into numbers.

There always was an opposition to the Kabbalah among the traditional rabbinical establishment. There is a famous story about Rabbi Saul Lieberman who, in response to students' explicit interest in studying the Kabbalah, referred to it as "nonsense", which does not deserve special lectures contrary to history of the Kabbalah, which does. One of the points raised in this context is the high status of the ten Sefirot, which bear similarity to the Christian trinity and may ultimately lead away from monotheism. This critique however is untenable as the Sefirot are concepts, not human or divine creatures.

As the other Jewish memes, the Kabbalah shows an extraordinary "infectious" capability. A somewhat anti-Semitic mutation of the term "Kabbalah" is the English word "cabal", which refers to a secretive group plotting against the existing order and hints at Jewish conspirators. Since the eighteenth century, kabalistic outlets have been found in various neo-pagan cults, astrology, and numerology. In recent years, the Kabbalah became a fashionable trend among gentiles, celebrities in particular. Mick Jagger, Demi Moore, Madonna, and Britney Spears are often mentioned as its pious followers; Madonna's recent visit to Israel has become a kabalistic show. In extreme cases, studies of the Kabbalah serve as a cover for commercial enterprise.

It seems that the famous character of *Frankenstein* created by Mary Shelley in the nineteenth century originated from the Jewish meme of *golem*. The word "gelem" means "raw material" in Hebrew; "golem", which is something like an animated creature-robot, is considered to be a product of human activity. Like Adam, a golem is made of mud, clay, or dust; since only God could create a human out of dust, the golem is far from being human; the golem is a stupid or dumb being, which is amenable to human control to a certain degree; he may however be dangerous and go wild. According to another interpretation, a golem may be constructed by purity of purpose and uttering the Name of God, with each letter representing and in charge of a proper organ. Legends maintain that prominent rabbis, making use of a kabalistic technique, could make golems to serve them. Usually, golems would not speak; they also neither ate nor drunk, though according to other legends they would eat just about everything, including bricks. In the fourth century C.E., Abba Ben Rav Hamma, a Babylonian merchant, better known as Rava, used his knowledge of the Kabbalah, in particular of the Sefer Yetzirah (Book of Creation), to create a humanized Golem. Since then, mystics have followed his steps, producing these creatures and claiming that the golems, by their very existence, demonstrate the validity of the Sefer Yetzirah.

The most famous golem is the Golem of Prague. In general, the Czech capital was home for numerous Jewish scholars. In 1850, Judah Loew, known as the Maharal of Praque, a great Rabbi and expert of the Kabbalah, made use of sticky clay from the banks of the Vltava River to create a golem specializing in protection of inhabitants of the ghetto against Czech violence, in particular, against the notorious priest, Taddeush, who had accused the Jews of ritual murder. Each night the Golem, who was exceptionally strong but far from brilliant, would get instructions about his duties on a piece of paper put in his mouth. In the morning, the Golem would go to sleep. The Golem's forehead was inscribed with the word "emet" meaning "truth" in Hebrew; this made him to obey the Rabbi's orders. The Golem could be destroyed by erasing the first letter of this word and thereby transforming the inscription into the word "met", which is "dead" in Hebrew. As the Golem grew bigger and stronger, he would often go wild. A deal was struck with the Czechs that violence against the Jews would stop if the Rabbi destroyed the Golem, which was done. Another account maintains that the Rabbi hid him in the attic of the famous Prague synagogue; the fact is that the statue of the Golem is still there, at the entrance of the old Jewish quarter of Prague.

Like the Eternal Jew, the golem has proven to be an enduring meme; it became a hero of novels, stories, cartoons, and plays in English, German, and Yiddish. In 1808, Jakob Grimm wrote a tale on a golem misused as house servant; Judah Low ben Bezalel wrote a series of tales about the golem, later developed by Gustav Meyrink into a novel *Der Golem* in 1915, and produced a movie series starring actor Paul Wegener. A TV-series *The X-Files* included an episode about a Hasidic woman employing a golem to avenge her husband's murder by neo-Nazis; J.R.R. Tolkien, the fantasy writer, used mass-manufactured golem-like creatures in his *Lord of the Rings* series. Recently, the Israeli newspaper *Yedioth Ahronoth* produced a comic strip with a golem depicted as a governmental super-hero resolving acute Israeli problems. The golem also appears in various video-games, such as *Pokemon*.

There are rabbis considering ghosts and spirits to be an integral part of Judaism. They point to the Old Testament which contains at least two references to the shamanic concept of *dybbuk*, which is a wandering and restless soul that sticks to a person and controls his or her behavior. In the Book of Samuel, a bad spirit adheres to King Saul; then in the Book of

Kings the soul of a dead man attaches itself to the prophet Elijah. The word "dybbuk" originates from the Hebrew *ledavek*, which means "to cling". A dybbuk usually attacks a person for a limited period of time and may bring about mental illnesses; sometimes a dybbuk may talk via the person's mouth. To expel the intruder, a rabbi may resort to various incantations and shamanic rituals, followed by blasts of the shofar, a ram's horn used as a musical instrument.

The role of Jews as authors and subjects of jokes is well-known. Anecdotes involving Jews are widely spread all over the world, illustrating once again the ability of memes to propagate from one person to another. Spicy sexual as well as political jokes were in fact a reaction of Diaspora Jews to hostile environment.

In the Soviet Union, telling a joke with political overtones was a risky business, and the storyteller could soon find himself under interrogation by the KGB (Soviet Secret Service in the post-war era); still, the temptation was too strong. Facing a cruel and corrupt regime, people were looking for human wit and mutual understanding, which a good gag could deliver. A famous series of such jokes, either sexual or political, was known as "Armenian Radio Broadcasts" and was widely believed to have been authored by Jews.

It seems that anti-Soviet political anecdotes were first introduced by Karl Radek in the twenties. He was born in Lviv, presently Ukraine, in 1885 to Jewish parents and grew up as a confused and passionate radical. After a stormy revolutionary career in Poland, Germany, and Russia, he disappeared in Stalin's prisons. Radek anticipated his tragic fate, when he commented: "Stalin and I disagree on the agricultural policy, he wants me buried under the ground, but I object". His other joke referred to Stalin's purges of the thirties which eliminated, among others, nearly all the Jewish members of the Politburo, the highest authority of the Communist Party. Radek compared Stalin with Moses: "Moses led Jews out of Egypt, Stalin from the Politburo".

In the United States, a stereotype of the Jewish American Princess (JAP) gave birth to a series of jokes. The JAP is a collective image of a spoiled Jewish girl, who grew up in a well-to-do American family, a sort of hothouse plant. Here is a typical example: what does a JAP make for a dinner? Reservations.

A jargon was another reaction of the discriminated Jewish minority. The meme of *shaygetz* (in Yiddish) usually referred to a young gentile man or teenager, who was perceived as non-educated and badly-mannered, if not wild. Anything could be expected of him. Having a non-Jewish girl-friend, *shiksa* in Yiddish, was a compensatory impulse for a Jewish man, a sort of sweet, forbidden fruit, brought about by centuries of isolation in ghettos. Shiksa is usually perceived as an experienced young female often ready to depart on a new adventure. In a recent book, Kristina Grish claims that a shiksa's status is presently considered cool and even fashionable, at least, in New York. Nevertheless, racist movements would regard a shiksa and her Jewish boyfriend as polluters of a pure genetic pool of the Aryan race.

The word "*goy*" (plural: *goyim*) simply means "non-Jew" in both Hebrew and Yiddish; unlike shiksa and shaygetz, it may be used without personification, merely a general term, implying a dichotomy between Jews and gentiles, between the Chosen People and the rest. This term does suggest a certain degree of polarity between the two. As a result, it was commonly perceived as derogatory and is presently considered as out-dated. The anti-Jewish interpretation of this word is "cattle", falsely suggesting the way Jews refer to gentiles. This word appears in the Bible many times merely meaning "nation" and, depending on the context, may refer to either Israelites or gentiles. In any case, the dichotomy results from the meme of the Covenant and has no genetic implications.

A purely Israeli contribution to Jewish memetics is a meme of *chutzpah*, which may mean audacity; there is difference of opinion about the origin of this word, whether it is Hebrew word, which later infected Yiddish, or the other way around. Regardless of its etymological roots, chutzpah is considered to be an attribute of the Israeli national character and may be traced to the traditional rebellious mentality of Jews. It may also follow from a more prosaic reason: lack of good manners. This word appears in dictionaries and is used by media; recently, it emerged in a verdict by the

United States Supreme Court to characterize a delicate dividing line between impudence and audaciousness.

Jewish Sex

Needless to say, the Jewish X and Y sex chromosomes, as can be seen from the previous chapter, are identical to those of gentiles; no definitive statistics is available to show that the Jewish sexual habits differ from those of gentiles. Thus, if there is anything "singular" about Jewish sex, it has to do with memes.

Kristina Grish, who published the first book devoted entirely to the phenomenon of shiksa, was the gentile girlfriend of numerous Jewish men and claims a close familiarity with the subject. As a shiksa, Grish is no pioneer; the meme, if extrapolated back to ancient times, can be traced to Moses, who was married to Zipporah, the daughter of Hobab, a pagan priest of Midian. She gave birth to their son, Gershom. Jews did not leave Moses in solitude; many other Jews had a soft spot for gentile women and followed in his steps, among them, King Solomon, a symbol of wealth and wisdom. He married ample set of pagan beauties; altogether he was said to have had seven hundred wives and three hundred concubines.

Nevertheless, the Bible cautioned that a shiksa may be fatal. Dalila, a Philistine and the wife of Samson, a Hebrew hero of Herculian status, left an ominous footprint in the Jewish national memory. Conspiring with Philistines, she first learnt that Samson's exceptional strength lay in his hair; when he was sleeping, she shaved the hair leaving him powerless. Philistines captured Samson and blinded him but, while in prison, his hair grew again as well as his strength. When summoned to entertain the enemy in their pagan temple, he pulled down the pillars with all his might, destroying the structure and killing the enemies and himself. His last words were "Let me die with the Philistines". This phrase is cited by admirers of the suicide bombers to sarcastically point out that the first suicidal killing in history was committed by a Jew.

Joseph Zuss (or Suss) Oppenheimer was an influential banker and financial adviser for Prince Karl Alexander von Wurttenberg of Stuttgart in the first half of the eighteenth century. Handsome and elegant Zuss enjoyed sexual favors of shiksas, in this case the court ladies, though his main expertise was in ruthless tax collection. These activities could not win him many friends and in fact had proven fatal. After the sudden death of his patron, he was arrested, heavily tortured and forced to confess to any possible crime. But he stubbornly refused the offer to convert. He was hanged as a Jew in 1738; there were persistent speculations that the Jew, Zuss, was, in fact, the illegitimate son of a German nobleman.

Leon Weuchtwanger described his extraordinary life and death in a novel "*Jew Zuss*". In 1940, the Nazis jumped the opportunity and produced a propaganda film under the same title with Werner Krauss, a talented actor, starring in the main role; a key scene displayed a brutal rape of innocent Christian girl. Hitler, fixated on the Jews polluting the Aryan genetic pool, ordered to confirm Krauss' status of Actor of the State.

With emancipation of the Jews in Europe and mass immigration to the United States, love affairs among Jewish men and **gentile** women became popular though not always disclosed. The Serbian Mileva Maric was Albert Einstein's shiksa, whom he later married. It would be tedious to go with the list.

Apparently, Marilyn Monroe was the most famous shiksa. Jewish directors, lawyers, psycho-analysts, and brokers dominated the Hollywood movie industry and made use of their influence to promote this or that actress in exchange for sex. Besides numerous straight affairs with men, many of them Jewish, Monroe was rumored to be involved with her Jewish personal manager Natasha Lytess. Later Monroe converted to Judaism in order to marry playwright Arthur Miller. The case of Marilyn Monroe is merely an illustration of what was going on in Hollywood at those times, even though, Scott Fitzgerald, the prominent American writer of the era (and a heavy drinker), was probably exaggerating, when he commented in this regard: "a Jewish holyday, a gentile tragedy".

The meme of shiksa, however interesting, reflects only one facet of the Jewish sexual mentality. In general, Judaism and Christianity view sex in opposite ways. The Christian meme of celibacy was copied by priests, monks, and nuns from Greek deities Athena, and Hestia; though the

motivation was different: the latter considered it a means of female liberation, the former as practice of refraining from sin. The sexual abstinence of
the deities could not have any genetic consequences, but the celibacy of
Catholic priests seems to limit propagation of genes responsible for intelligence and discipline they are supposed to possess. Celibacy is an explicit
illustration of how memes may affect our genes. The official versions of
the Gospels maintain that Jesus was also unmarried, highly unusual for an
observant Jew at those times. He had special relations with Mary
Magdalena, who was first described as a prostitute and then as a saint. Subsequent literary versions even represented her as the secret wife of Jesus.

Unlike Christianity, the main streams of Judaism consider sex as a joyful way to procreate; satisfying sex between a husband and his wife is a
mitzvah, in other words, a positive deed carried out of the religious com-
mitment; it is in compliance with the Ten Commandments. Rabbis
declared the erotic poem *Song of Songs*, attributed to King Solomon, as
holy. Though monogamy was accepted as the ideal, the Bible and the Talmud tolerated polygamy. The cases of polygamy were recorded among
Spanish Jews as late as the fourteenth century.

The Talmud speaks about the principle of *Pru Urvu*, which means "be
fruitful and multiply", but restricted the number of legitimate wives to
four that was later adopted by the Koran. Sex must be kept within the
frameworks of marriage. Any out-of-wedlock sexual activity, even that
short of intercourse, is explicitly forbidden. Judaism sees sexual intercourse
as a meaningful event for the both parties involved and uses the word "to
know" in order to describe this experience. Male masturbation and sexual
relations between men are strictly forbidden; the latter is punishable by
death. By way of contrast, the Talmud is vague about female homosexuality and permits birth control and abortion under certain circumstances.
Orthodox Jews practice physical separation during the woman's menstrual
period. At the end of this period, a woman must immerse herself in a ritual
pool, the so-called *mikvah*, though the idea behind this ceremony has to
do more with religious purification than with physical cleanliness. In
1999, Rabbi Shmuley Boteach published a book on kosher sex.

Since the ancient times up to these days, as could be expected, Jews did not exactly follow these prescriptions. Even King David, the national hero and a symbol of Jewish strength and wisdom, gave in to temptation. The Bible elaborated David's adultery with Bathsheba, the wife of his soldier, Uriah the Hittite. David already had seven wives; still, when he noticed Bathsheba when she was bathing; he decided to bring her to his chambers and they had sex. Then he arranged for Uriah to be killed in a battle and Bathsheba became his eighth wife. David and Bathsheba were therefore punished by God: their first child died at age of seven days.

As I noted earlier, genetic tests evidence a high degree of attachment of Jewish women to Jewish men, at least for procreation; if there was sex with gentiles, however passionate and satisfying, it left only a minor genetic signature per generation. The famous affair between Monica Lewinsky, a young White House employee, and President Bill Clinton, which was for whatever reasons exclusively focused on fellatio, belongs in this category. Jewish women were always popular among nobility, especially in Spain and Arab countries. Despite the mass Jewish emigration from Morocco to Israel, the late Moroccan King Hassan II patronized the Moroccan Jews, who still feel a deep admiration for him. He liked Jewish women, in particular young and beautiful. There is little doubt that sex between Jews and gentiles is no less frequent and variable than sex among other ethnic groups.

Presumably, the ethnicity is of minor concern for a prostitute and her client. The story has it that David Ben-Gurion, as a secular national leader, viewed the appearance of prostitutes on streets of Tel Aviv as a healthy phenomenon: at last, the Jews were becoming a "normal" nation. He was naïve, as a Jewish whore was never a rarity. Since prostitution is a pattern of human behavior, which involves copying and propagation from one individual to another, it may be treated from a memetic point of view.

Prostitution was a basic theme in the Scriptures and considered as sinful as idolatry. In particular, inhabitants of the Northern Kingdom idolized Baal, the Canaanite god of fertility, and promiscuity was widely spread there. That is why Assyrians succeeded in destroying the kingdom, as the Bible suggested. Hosea foresaw God's reprisals in his prophecies; his marriage to Gomer, a whore, scrutinized in detail in the Bible, was to symbolize the chance for redemption offered by the Covenant between God and the Jews.

Jews produced a spectacular row of Madams. A case which exploded in the nineties involved Heidi Fleiss, a young, attractive brunette and the daughter of a respected Los Angeles pediatrician. After a short introductory course into "the world's oldest profession", the energetic Heidi started her own business; she provided top prostitutes for international businessmen and Hollywood stars and managed to make a fortune. Her success was so well-known that police assembled a task force to stop the festival. Posing as wealthy Japanese, an undercover police officer arranged for four girls to arrive at his hotel for $6,000. When the women explicitly agreed to have sex and were recorded, no less than twenty agents burst into the room and arrested them. Heidi followed the next day; she was accused of pandering, tax evasion, possession of narcotics, and money laundering. As her clientele included famous movie personalities and financial moguls, the scandal that erupted could have developed epic proportions, but Madam Heidi wisely kept her mouth shut. After serving her prison term, she worked as a sex tips advisor on a Web site and published a book in the field of her expertise straightforwardly entitled "*Pandering*".

Presently, Heidi is busy with a new enterprise: a male brothel in which men cater to women. As reported by the media, her partner elaborated what they have in mind: "Say, a guy gets into an argument with his wife. What does he do? Lot of times, he goes out, gets a drink, goes to a place to be serviced. Now women can say "Hey, if you can do it, I can too". Her other modest ambition is building a brothel in Nevada, USA, which would be a precise replica of the White House. As a teenager, Heidi was well-known in her neighborhood as a careful trusted babysitter and a superb chess player.

4

The Magic Loop

All things are mortal but the Jew, all forces pass, but he remains. What is the secret of his immortality?

—Mark Twain

Each nation is unique in its own way. Is it possible to make sense of Jewish uniqueness as described in this book?

Unlike gender or hair color, Jewish "otherness" is not a genetic trait, and therefore the key to the understanding of Jewish people lies with their memes. Nearly all of them rely on the presumption of the Covenant. The circumstances of the very event of this unparalleled contract between the universal and all-mighty Divine authority, the absolute perfection, and an ethnic group of mortal and sinful human beings, remain a mystery. In this sense the Jewish singularity lacks a rational basis. Nevertheless, after a few millennia, it shows no signs of decay which seems to say something about human nature.

The Covenant has always been the monumental substrate underlying the Jewish identity. Breath-taking compositions of the modern Israeli video artist, Michal Rovner, combine the two polar elements in a single artifact: an eternal and enormous, on the one hand, and a fluid and diminutive, struggling to survive, on the other. Her video composition *"Tablets"* appears to reflect the mystery of the Covenant in a particularly sophisticated way. The two illuminated rectangular stone tablets of a considerable size are placed on a sand ground, symbolizing the everlasting foundation. The ordered series of small letters are projected on their rough surfaces. Under a closer look, one can detect that the "letters" are in fact tiny human figures trying with all their might to perform a concerted motion on the tablet's surface. The full spectrum of the Jewish experience in Diaspora is expressed in colorful and highly emotional paintings of Mark Chagall.

Though the mystery behind the Covenant remains unresolved, its consequences can be put into a rational framework. Take, for example, the Egyptians who created a glorious civilization, as ancient as the Jewish one; they remained settled in the same territory for a period of several millennia, adjusting their religion, culture, and language as demanded by their surrounding. As a result, there is a fundamental disparity between the ancient and modern Egyptians. The latter worship a different God and speak a different language. The Jews were quite the opposite: they also began very early but for a period of two millennia were on a constant move to preserve their soul at any cost. The Promised Land was largely maintained as the concept, the core meme. Believing in their unique destiny, the Chosen People did their best to stay mentally close to the host population without sacrificing the charters of their precious Covenant, the very heart of their identity. They often failed, so that their mental posture and obvious ambitions often aroused deep animosity and, as a result, the Jews moved on.

The very process of changing the environment and the surrounding culture stimulates imagination, learning, and adaptation; any immigrant knows this very well. Merely acquiring a new language may amount to a new perception of the world. A smooth, calm and ordered way of life is frequently the best medication against creativity. Mobility further reinforced the Jewish potential as survivors. This process repeated itself for centuries.

It seems that I can represent it by the loop shown in Figure 5 below. Consisting of the four indispensable links, it displays what is known in engineering as a closed system which may support itself without external intervention. It starts from the presumption of the Chosen People shown at the top and bottom of the loop, giving rise to animosity on the part of a host and thereby forcing Jews to move. This in turn supports survival, which again feeds the hostility of a host and forces Jews to migrate.

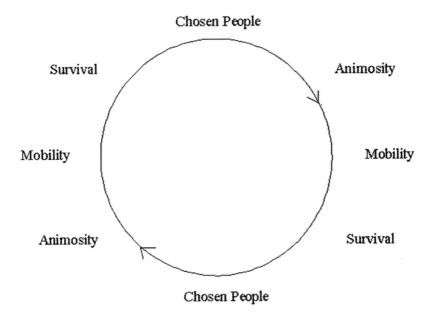

Figure 5. Loop of Jewish Experience in Diaspora.
*No rational explanation for the presumption of Covenant
and Chosen People is available.*

The cases of the two prominent scientists, Hermann Muller, a geneticist, and Arno Penzias, a physicist, described earlier, provide a good illustration for the efficiency of the loop. They grew up in a multi-cultural and competitive environment, were sensitive to social issues, rebellious, mobile and highly ambitious. In short, according to a Jewish recipe, they had all the components needed for success.

Thus, we do have a rational explanation for the three links of the loop: mobility, survival, and animosity, typical of the Jewish experience. But where did the presumption of the "chosen people", the fourth, vital link, come from?

There is a major problem with rational explanations of the very event of the Covenant; its origins are a complete mystery, unless we adopt the Biblical story of divine intervention. This is especially disappointing, as this link serves as the battery, which sets the loop in rotation. William James, a prominent American psychologist, once noted: "I myself believe that the evidence for God lies primarily in inner personal experiences". If this is so, what was the personal experience that motivated the ancient Hebrews to make their choice for YHWH among all other possibilities available at the time? If the Covenant, which is a source of both Jewish greatness and Jewish tragedy, is a myth, how is it that such an intelligent tribe, paying a terrible price, would believe it for such a long period of time with such intense passion?

We should bear in mind that this crucial event took place several millennia ago, when other people were worshipping multiple idols which were fed and, in many cases, dressed by humans. Local kings, among them Egyptian pharaohs, were considered to be living gods. For a pagan, something must be seen in order to exist; deities must be specialized, each in its own field, to be capable of performing their narrowly defined duties. Paganism survives up to these days. A recent media report on a Malaysian sect idolizing a giant tea kettle provides fresh evidence.

Praying to an all-mighty, universal, single, but unobservable God was a revolution of cosmic proportions, a sort of spiritual Big Bang. The concept was both the maximum of abstraction and the maximum of simplicity. Such a god anticipates imagination and intelligence from a believer, the qualities ancient Hebrews apparently possessed for unknown reasons. Besides the Bible, we have no account of the causes and circumstances of this dramatic breakthrough which was destined to reshape the world.

Physicians have noted that innocent sugar pills, declared as a powerful medication did indeed alleviate a patient's symptoms; this treatment is reported as particularly efficient against painful sensations, in which the brain generates a pattern of neural activity resulting in quantifiable analgesia. This is known as the *placebo* effect, embodied in human physiology: a patient believes in the mightiness of the pills, so they work to spark the appropriate biochemical processes. We may speculate that something similar happened to the Jews: they believed they were the Chosen People, so they became such. There is also the polar, *nocebo* effect: a skeptic patient renders his conditions worse. Gentiles, who think of themselves as nothing special, fulfill their expectations. Both of these phenomena worked in opposite directions at the same time and may well be responsible for a mental difference between Jews and gentiles.

Thus, it is possible to rationalize consequences of the Covenant, not the mere event. Was there a Divine intervention or not? Who is the author of the Bible? For many decades historians have claimed that it is a product of mortal humans, which bears no proof of supernatural interference. Jews on the other hand have long insisted that the Torah was given to Moses by God in the most direct and unambiguous way. The Vilna Gaon wrote in his "*The Book of Hidden Things*": "The rule is that all that was, is, and will be until the end of time is included in the Torah from "*Bereishit*" (the first verse of Genesis) to "*L'eynei kol Yisrael*" (the last verse of Deuteronomy). And not merely in a general sense, but including the details of every species and of each person individually, and the minutest details of everything that happened to him from the day of his birth until his death." The Hebrew language is a special gift from God and is sacred.

It took a truly unique personality such as that of Slovakian Rabbi Michael Dov Weissmandel to discover a new angle of looking at the divinity of the Bible. He was a Torah scholar and mathematician with a particular passion for codes and ciphers. During the Second World War, he managed to escape from a train to Auschwitz using a small saw that he had earlier concealed, with the skills of an experienced convict, in a slice of bread. One day, already in New-York, Weissmandel decided to search for a possible Biblical encoding of the word "Torah" which, in Hebrew, consists of four letters: Tav, Vav, Reish and Hey. As the Torah was given by God fifty days after the Jews left Egypt, Weissmandel assumed that he should look for a code which employs an interval of each fifty letters. He opened the first book of the Bible, Genesis, and circled the first Tav, which he spotted, then he skipped fifty letters and indeed encountered the letter Vav; going on and skipping fifty letters once again he found Reish and then, in the same way, the last letter, Hey. Thus, the word "Torah" was indeed hidden beneath the surface of the holy text. Amazingly, he found the same code in the book of Exodus. This became known as the equidistant letter sequences (ELSs) or equally spaced letters. You may want to practice with the text of Genesis a fragment of which is given in Appendix C.

If codes are indeed there, they would be evidence for Divine intervention, but Weissmandel died in 1957, without his striking finds having gotten much attention. The breakthrough came in 1994, when a team of Israeli mathematicians, Eliyahu Rips, Doron Witztum and Yoav Rosenberg, published a paper in the respectable, peer-reviewed *Journal of Statistical Science*, entitled "*Equidistant Letter Sequences in the Book of Genesis*". The paper dealt with a computer program, known as the "rabbis experiment", which would scan the book of Genesis for the hidden names of thirty two Jewish rabbis who had lived between the ninth and eighteenth centuries. The results confirmed not only most of the names of these rabbis but also the Hebrew dates of their birth and death encoded close to their names. The above code found by Weissmandel was also substantiated. The scientists calculated that the random chance of finding these combinations in close textual proximity were one in three million, in other words, they were deliberately planted there. Given the fact that the involved rabbis lived many centuries after the text was written, (the Qumran Scrolls were written around the first century B.C.E.), one should inescapably conclude about Divine origin of the book. It seemed that these discoveries have finally resolved the crucial issue regarding the origins of the Covenant, pointing to Divine intervention. But not so fast!

The book by Michael Drosnin, "*The Bible Code*", published in 1997, became a best-seller but went far beyond the original research of the Israelis and drew much criticism from professionals. The author claimed that, among other things, Edison's invention of the light bulb, Shakespeare's writing "*Hamlet*", and Jack Ruby's shooting Lee Harvey Oswald, were all encoded in the Bible. He did not stop there as the assassination of Israeli Prime Minister Yitzhak Rabin was also inscribed in the "sub-text". Mathematician Brendan McKay ridiculed these findings by demonstrating that it was possible to locate the assassination of Indian Prime Minister Indira Gandhi encoded in the text of "*Moby Dick*", as well as that of John Kennedy, Leon Trotsky, and even of Michael Drosnin himself! McKay and his colleagues published a paper in 1999, which showed that the original "rabbi experiment" by the Israeli team contained a sort of implicit tuning of the algorithm. Computer whiz, Don Steinberg, commented that

"Whenever powerful computers, large documents, and people with a whole lot of free time are involved, anything is possible". He applied an algorithm similar to the "rabbis experiment" to a Microsoft software license agreement and discovered there, among other things, an encoded description of boxer Mike Tyson biting Evander Holyfield's ear! The situation was more complicated with the Torah: depending on the edition, there are slight differences in the texts, which may be sufficient to violate or, alternatively, further support the code; the Hebrew alphabet consists of consonants, allowing for further liberties with vowels.

Yet, this brilliant criticism does not prove that these or other codes are not present in the Bible. They may well be there and may have remained either misunderstood or still hidden. After all, the Magic Loop itself may also follow from Divine intervention.

The dispute about the origins of the Bible is still open. Having in mind the basic Jewish stipulation that God is not a part of this world but is its creator keeping the cards "close to his chest", we can safely assume that the controversy can hardly be resolved.

Additional Reading

I History

Armstrong, K. *A History of God*. New York: Gramercy Book, 1993.

Churchill, W. S. *Zionism versus Bolshevism*, The Illustrated Sunday Herald, February 8, 1920.

Della Pergola, S. *A Question of Numbers*, www.haaretz.com, January, 2006. http://www.haaretz.com/hasen/spages/674640.html

Dershowitz, A. *The Case for Israel*, New York: Wiley, 2003.

Drosnin, M. *The Bible Code*. New York: Simon & Schuster, 1997.

Drosnin, M. *Bible Code II: The Countdown*. New York: Viking, 2002.

Ecker R. *The Bible Code Hits a Bumpy Road*, http://www.hobrad.com/acrebibl.htm, 2003

Elon, A. *The Pity of It All, A Portrait of the German-Jewish Epoch: 1743–1933*. New York: Picador, 2002.

Haskins, M. *Drugs, A User's Guide*, Sydney: Random House, 2003.

Johnson, P. *A History of the Jews*, New York: Harper & Row, 1987.

Krauthammer, C. The Weekly Standard, May 11, 1998.

Nasar, S. *A Beautiful Mind*, New York: Touchstone Book, 1998.

Rigg, B. M. *Hitler's Jewish Soldiers*, Lawrence: University Press of Kansas, 2004.

Rockaway, R. A. *But He Was Good to His Mother*, Jerusalem: Gefen, 2000.

Shirer, W. L. *Rise and Fall of the Third Reich*, New York: Simon & Schuster, 1990.

Solzhenitsyn, A. *Two Hundred Years Together*. (in Russian: Dvesti Let Vmeste), Part I, Moscow: Russkiy Put, 2001.

Solzhenitsyn, A. *Two Hundred Years Together*, (in Russian: Dvesti Let Vmeste), Part II, Moscow: Russkiy Put, 2002.

Witztum, D., Rips, E. and Rosenberg, Y. *Equidistant Letter Sequences in the Book of Genesis. Statistical Science* 9(3), 429–438, 1994 (abridged).

Yos, N. *On Joining the Jews*, Commentary, March 2004.

II Genes

Cochran, G., Hardy, J., Harpending, H. *Natural History of Ashkenazi Intelligence*, 2005. http://harpend.dsl.xmission.com/Documents/AshkenaziIQ.jbiosocsci.pdf

Dawkins, R. *The Selfish Gene*, Oxford: Oxford Univ Press, 1989.

Hamer, D. *The God Gene: How Faith Is Hardwired Into Our Genes*, New York: Doubleday, 2004.

Kleiman, Y. *DNA and Tradition: The Genetic Link to Ancient Hebrews*, New York: Devora, 2004.

Lewis, R. *Human Genetics: Concepts and Application*, Boston: McGraw Hill, 2005.

Margulis, L. and Sagan, D. *Acquiring Genomes*, New York: Basic Books, 2003.

Olsen, S. *Mapping Human History: Genes, Race, and Our Common Origins*, Boston: Houghton-Mifflin, 2002.

Relethford, J. H. *Reflections of Our Past: How Human History is Revealed in Our Genes*. Boulder: Westview Press, 2003.

Ridley, M. *Genome*, New York: Perennial, 2000,

III Memes

Berg, P. S. *Kabbalah for the Layman*. Jerusalem: Press of the Research Center for Kabbalah, 1984.

Boteach, S. *Kosher Sex*. New York: Doubleday, 1999.

Cornell, E. *What Was God Thinking? Science Can't Tell*. Time, November 14, 2005.

Golan, A. *Hodaya, Ateret Malchut, Come Home This Minute!* www.haaretz.com. August, 2005.

Grish, K. *Boy Vey! The Shiksa's Guide for Dating Jewish Men*. New York: Simon Spotlight Entertainment, 2005.

Hale, C. *Himmler's Crusade: The Nazi Expedition to Find the Origins Of the Aryan Race*. New York: Wiley, 2003.

Handwerker, H. *Jewish, Yes. American, Yes. But am I a Princess?* www.haaretz.com. June, 2006.

Hubler, S. *Fleiss Plans a Brothel to Serve Women*. Los Angeles Times, November 17, 2005.

Livneh, N. *Messianic Mania*. www.haaretz.com. December, 2005.

Minkoff, D. *The Ultimate Book of Jewish Jokes*. London: Robson Books, 2005.

Nasar, S., *A Beautiful Mind*. New York: Touchstone Book, 1998.

Singh, S. *Big Bang*, New York: Fourth Estate, 2004.

Shragai, N. *In the Beginning was Al-Aqsa*. www.haaretz.com, November 2005.

Taylor, J. *When the Clock Struck Zero*. New York: St. Martins Press, 1993.

APPENDIX A

Jewish Calendar

Today is the 4-th of October 2005, by the Jewish calendar it is the 1-st of Tishrei, 5766; this date coincides with a Jewish New Year; the date of the next Jewish New Year is 23 September 2006, by the Jewish calendar it is the 1-st of Tishrei, 5767. As you can see the two calendars, Gregorian and Jewish, are different.

The Jewish calendar has the following months:

Jewish Month	Number	Length	Gregorian Equivalent
Nissan	1	30 days	March-April
Iyar	2	29 days	April-May
Sivan	3	30 days	May-June
Tammuz	4	29 days	June-July
Av	5	30 days	July-August
Elul	6	29 days	August-September
Tishrei	7	30 days	September-October
Cheshvan	8	29 or 30 days	October-November
Kislev	9	30 or 29 days	November-December
Tevet	10	29 days	December-January
Shevat	11	30 days	January-February
Adar I (for leap years only)	12	30 days	February-March
Adar (referred to as Adar II in leap years)	12 (13 in leap years)	29 days	February-March

This calendar is basically lunar; in ancient times, a new month began with the first sight of moon's sliver; if confirmed by several independent observers, the Sanhedrin would announce first of the month. Consequently, the Jewish year differs from a solar year on the Gregorian calendar and has a variable "duration". Note that the Gregorian calendar did not exist until the sixteenth century. The dates of Jewish holidays do not change from year to year by the Jewish calendar, but they do by the Gregorian one.

Every solar year contains roughly 12.4 lunar months, implying that a 13-month lunar year lasts nearly 19 days more and 12-month lunar is 11 days shorter; there is a relative shift. For example, the month of Nissan occurs 11 days earlier each Gregorian year, traveling through the Spring, Winter, Fall, and Summer, and then the Spring again; so an extra month would be occasionally added to make up for the "drift": a second month of Adar. To avoid the uncontrolled accumulation of the disparity between the two calendars, in the fourth century the length of months and the addition of month was standardized over the period of a 19 year cycle: Adar II is added in the 3rd, 6th, 8th, 11th, 14th, 17th and 19th years of this cycle. The present cycle began October 2, 1997 that corresponds to the Jewish year 5758. Because of religious limitations, a day is subtracted from the month of Kislev or is added to the month of Cheshvan of the next year.

The Jewish calendar begins to count the year number from the time of creation by adding up the ages of people appearing in the Bible. The first month and the Jewish New Year are not the same; Nissan is the first month, the New Year is celebrated in Tishrei, the seventh month.

Note that Adar has 30 days in leap years and 29 days in non-leap years. Many computer programs can be easily accessed to calculate the Jewish calendar for a century ahead.

APPENDIX B

Conversion of Hebrew Letters into Numbers

Glyph	Hebrew	Decimal
א	*Aleph,*	1
ב	*Bet,*	2
ג	*Gimmel,*	3
ד	*Dalet*	4
ה	*He*	5
ו	*Vav*	6
ז	*Zayin*	7
ח	*Het*	8
ט	*Tet*	9
י	*Yod*	10
כ	*Kaf*	20
ל	*Lamed*	30
מ	*Mem*	40
נ	*Nun*	50
ס	*Samekh*	60
ע	*Ayin*	70
פ	*Pe*	80
צ	*Tsadi*	90
ק	*Kof*	100
ר	*Resh*	200
ש	*Shin*	300
ת	*Tav*	400
ק"ת or ך	*Tav Kof* or *Kaf Sofit*	500
ר"ת or ם	*Tav Resh* or *Mem Sofit*	600
ש"ת or ן	*Tav Shin* or *Nun Sofit*	700
ת"ת or ף	*Tav Tav* or *Pe Sofit*	800
ק"תת or ץ	*Tav Tav Kof* or *Tsadi Sofit*	900

APPENDIX C

Fragment of the Book of Genesis

בְּרֵאשִׁית, בָּרָא אֱ־לֹהִים, אֵת הַשָּׁמַיִם, וְאֵת הָאָרֶץ. **ב** וְהָאָרֶץ, הָיְתָה תֹהוּ וָבֹהוּ, וְחֹשֶׁךְ, עַל-פְּנֵי תְהוֹם; וְרוּחַ אֱ־לֹהִים, מְרַחֶפֶת עַל-פְּנֵי הַמָּיִם. **ג** וַיֹּאמֶר אֱ־לֹהִים, יְהִי אוֹר; וַיְהִי-אוֹר. **ד** וַיַּרְא אֱ־לֹהִים אֶת-הָאוֹר, כִּי-טוֹב; וַיַּבְדֵּל אֱ־לֹהִים, בֵּין הָאוֹר וּבֵין הַחֹשֶׁךְ. **ה** וַיִּקְרָא אֱ־לֹהִים לָאוֹר יוֹם, וְלַחֹשֶׁךְ קָרָא לָיְלָה; וַיְהִי-עֶרֶב וַיְהִי-בֹקֶר, יוֹם אֶחָד.

וַיֹּאמֶר אֱ־לֹהִים, יְהִי רָקִיעַ בְּתוֹךְ הַמָּיִם, וִיהִי מַבְדִּיל, בֵּין מַיִם לָמָיִם. **ז** וַיַּעַשׂ אֱ־לֹהִים, אֶת-הָרָקִיעַ, וַיַּבְדֵּל בֵּין הַמַּיִם אֲשֶׁר מִתַּחַת לָרָקִיעַ, וּבֵין הַמַּיִם אֲשֶׁר מֵעַל לָרָקִיעַ; וַיְהִי-כֵן. **ח** וַיִּקְרָא אֱ־לֹהִים לָרָקִיעַ, שָׁמָיִם; וַיְהִי-עֶרֶב וַיְהִי-בֹקֶר, יוֹם שֵׁנִי.

וַיֹּאמֶר אֱ־לֹהִים, יִקָּווּ הַמַּיִם מִתַּחַת הַשָּׁמַיִם אֶל-מָקוֹם אֶחָד, וְתֵרָאֶה, הַיַּבָּשָׁה; וַיְהִי-כֵן. **י** וַיִּקְרָא אֱ־לֹהִים לַיַּבָּשָׁה אֶרֶץ, וּלְמִקְוֵה הַמַּיִם קָרָא יַמִּים; וַיַּרְא אֱ־לֹהִים, כִּי-טוֹב. **יא** וַיֹּאמֶר אֱ־לֹהִים, תַּדְשֵׁא הָאָרֶץ דֶּשֶׁא עֵשֶׂב מַזְרִיעַ זֶרַע, עֵץ פְּרִי עֹשֶׂה פְּרִי לְמִינוֹ, אֲשֶׁר זַרְעוֹ-בוֹ עַל-הָאָרֶץ; וַיְהִי-כֵן. **יב** וַתּוֹצֵא הָאָרֶץ דֶּשֶׁא עֵשֶׂב מַזְרִיעַ זֶרַע, לְמִינֵהוּ, וְעֵץ עֹשֶׂה-פְּרִי אֲשֶׁר זַרְעוֹ-בוֹ, לְמִינֵהוּ; וַיַּרְא אֱ־לֹהִים, כִּי-טוֹב. **יג** וַיְהִי-עֶרֶב וַיְהִי-בֹקֶר, יוֹם שְׁלִישִׁי.

וַיֹּאמֶר אֱ־לֹהִים, יְהִי מְאֹרֹת בִּרְקִיעַ הַשָּׁמַיִם, לְהַבְדִּיל, בֵּין הַיּוֹם וּבֵין הַלָּיְלָה; וְהָיוּ לְאֹתֹת וּלְמוֹעֲדִים, וּלְיָמִים וְשָׁנִים. **טו** וְהָיוּ לִמְאוֹרֹת בִּרְקִיעַ הַשָּׁמַיִם, לְהָאִיר עַל-הָאָרֶץ; וַיְהִי-כֵן. **טז** וַיַּעַשׂ אֱ־לֹהִים, אֶת-שְׁנֵי הַמְּאֹרֹת הַגְּדֹלִים: אֶת-הַמָּאוֹר הַגָּדֹל, לְמֶמְשֶׁלֶת הַיּוֹם, וְאֶת-הַמָּאוֹר הַקָּטֹן לְמֶמְשֶׁלֶת הַלַּיְלָה, וְאֵת הַכּוֹכָבִים. **יז** וַיִּתֵּן אֹתָם אֱ־לֹהִים, בִּרְקִיעַ הַשָּׁמָיִם, לְהָאִיר, עַל-הָאָרֶץ. **יח** וְלִמְשֹׁל, בַּיּוֹם וּבַלַּיְלָה, וּלְהַבְדִּיל, בֵּין הָאוֹר וּבֵין הַחֹשֶׁךְ; וַיַּרְא אֱ־לֹהִים, כִּי-טוֹב. **יט** וַיְהִי-עֶרֶב וַיְהִי-בֹקֶר, יוֹם רְבִיעִי.

וַיֹּאמֶר אֱ־לֹהִים--יִשְׁרְצוּ הַמַּיִם, שֶׁרֶץ נֶפֶשׁ חַיָּה; וְעוֹף יְעוֹפֵף עַל-הָאָרֶץ, עַל-פְּנֵי רְקִיעַ הַשָּׁמָיִם. **כא** וַיִּבְרָא אֱ־לֹהִים, אֶת-הַתַּנִּינִם הַגְּדֹלִים; וְאֵת כָּל-נֶפֶשׁ הַחַיָּה הָרֹמֶשֶׂת אֲשֶׁר שָׁרְצוּ הַמַּיִם לְמִינֵהֶם, וְאֵת כָּל-עוֹף כָּנָף לְמִינֵהוּ, וַיַּרְא אֱ־לֹהִים, כִּי-טוֹב. **כב** וַיְבָרֶךְ אֹתָם אֱ־לֹהִים, לֵאמֹר: פְּרוּ וּרְבוּ, וּמִלְאוּ אֶת-הַמַּיִם בַּיַּמִּים, וְהָעוֹף, יִרֶב בָּאָרֶץ. **כג** וַיְהִי-עֶרֶב וַיְהִי-בֹקֶר, יוֹם חֲמִישִׁי.

Glossary

Allele	One of two or more alternative forms of a gene having the same locus on homologous chromosomes and responsible for alternative traits.
Centromere	A specialized condensed region of each chromosome that appears during mitosis.
Chromosome	A threadlike body in the nucleus of the cell carrying the genes in a certain order.
Cytoplasm	The living substance of a cell excluding the nucleus.
Diaspora	The Jewish communities outside Palestine or modern Israel.
Diploid	A cell or organism having two sets of chromosomes or twice the haploid number.
Enzymes	Proteins that are produced by cells and act as catalysts in biochemical reactions.
Fungus	A parasitic plant reproducing by spores. It lacks leaves, true stems, and roots.
Gamete	A sexual reproductive cell which has a single set of unpaired chromosomes.
Genotype	A particular alleles composition or a group of organisms having a specific genetic composition.
Haploid	A cell or organism that has only one complete set of chromosomes.

Meiosis	Cell division which produces sex cells in sexually reproducing organisms: the nucleus divides into four nuclei each containing half the chromosome number.
Mitochondria	An organelle that contains enzymes responsible for producing energy.
Mitosis	Cell division: the nucleus divides into nuclei containing the same number of chromosomes.
Mold	A fungus producing a superficial growth on organic substances or damp.
Monotheism	Belief in a single and all-mighty God.
Nucleus	A part of the cell that contains DNA and RNA and is responsible for reproduction and growth.
Paganism	Belief in multiple gods; various religions other than Christianity or Judaism or Islam.
Phage	A parasitic virus that resides in bacteria; it uses the bacterium's machinery to produce more and more phage.
Phenotype	A consequence of the genotype; what an organism looks like. In a more general sense, a trait.
Proteins	A group of organic compounds consisting of polymers of amino acids. They are essential components of living cells.
Symbiosis	The relation between two different interdependent organisms; usually, each benefits from the other.
Zygote	The cell that results from the fusion of an ovum and a spermatozoon.

Index

978-0-595-40625-8
0-595-40625-4

Printed in the United States
123362LV00002BA/279/A

9 780595 406258